GREENING MODERNISM

GREENING
MODERNISM

Preservation,
Sustainability,
and the
Modern Movement

CARL STEIN

W.W. NORTON & COMPANY
New York · London

Manufacturing by KHL Printing Co. Pte Ltd
Book design by Guenet Abraham
Production manager: Leeann Graham
Digital production manager: J. Lops

Library of Congress Cataloging-in-Publication Data

Stein, Carl
 Greening modernism : preservation, sustainability, and
the modern movement / Carl Stein. — 1st ed.
   p. cm.
 Includes bibliographical references and index.
 ISBN 978-0-393-73283-2 (hardcover)
1. Sustainable architecture. 2. Sustainable buildings.
3. Modern movement (Architecture)—Conservation and
restoration. 4. Historic preservation. I. Title. II. Title:
Preservation, sustainability, and the modern movement.
 NA2542.36.S75 2010
 720'.47—dc22
                                                    2009050458

ISBN: 978-0-393-73283-2

W. W. Norton & Company, Inc.,
500 Fifth Avenue, New York, N.Y. 10110
www.wwnorton.com
W. W. Norton & Company Ltd.,
Castle House, 75/76 Wells Street,
London W1T 3QT

0 9 8 7 6 5 4 3 2 1

Acknowledgments

There are many, perhaps hundreds of people whose involvement over the years has been instrumental to the evolution of the attitudes and materials in this book. I am grateful to all; however, a few require special note.

Greening Modernism would not have occurred without the initial impetus and patient, early editing of Kristen Holt-Browning. Nancy Green provided final editing and, in particular, invaluable attention to detail and form. The thoughtful and elegant book design by Guenet Abraham is evident throughout the pages. Elemental Architectural and Sine Elemental created the environment and made time for this project, in particular, my partners Tom Abraham and John Barboni as well as Shira Rosan and Michelle Black, who have been here since the beginning.

My understanding and practice of architecture has been strongly shaped by the experience of working first for Marcel Breuer and his partners Ham Smith, Tician Papachristou, Bob Gatje, and Herb Beckhard, and then for Richard Stein, later my partner for thirteen years. My work continues to be informed by the decades of conversation and collaboration with sculptor Tino Nivola and painter Dan Kleeman.

Above all are the inspiration and support of three generations of family: Ethel and Nancy Stein and Jesse Lee Denning, to whom this book is dedicated.

Unless otherwise noted, all photographs are by the author or from the archives of The Stein Partnership/Elemental Architecture. Photographs noted MBA/GPS are from the archives of Marcel Breuer Associates and its successor firm, Gatje Papachristou Smith.

Contents

Introduction

Modern architecture, preservation of existing buildings, and sustainable design are inextricably interconnected threads that form a major strand within the larger fabric of an integrated worldview. Key to this view is the concern that resources be applied at their highest and best use, and that current decisions consider, as a primary criterion, their impact on future generations.

This book presents an architectural perspective. That is to say, despite frequent asides to relate the processes and technologies under discussion to the global ecostructure, the emphasis is on building design and on urban and regional planning. Although the focus is architecture and examples deal with the design and upgrade of buildings and communities, the set of attitudes that underlie a Modernist approach to the development of a sustainable built environment can be extended to virtually all areas of physical planning and resource allocation. This is not a catalog of specific techniques and technologies, but rather a discussion of the issues that have generated the multiple interlocking crises facing us today, and an analysis of a set of attitudes and processes that can and should

become the foundation for comprehensive solutions. Where individual techniques are presented, they serve as the bases for illustrating broader issues. Similarly, case studies that describe the relationships among specifically applied multiple technologies demonstrate the synergies achieved through their interactivity as well as the performance characteristics of the individual measures. The studies discuss why these phenomena occur, but they do not propose universal solutions.

While the primary intention of the book is to provide the broad understandings that will support the development of project-specific, creative solutions, it also includes quantitative material necessary to make informed judgments at both the micro and macro levels.

Throughout this book, Modern, Modernist, or Modernism, capitalized, indicate a reference to work or theory having broad substantive bases such as the Modern movement of the Congrès Internationaux d'Architecture Moderne (CIAM), the Bauhaus, or the Le Corbusier of *Vers une architecture*. The term *modern style* in lowercase refers to a body of work

or ideas whose generally understood characteristics are based on an a priori style or appearance, detached from any underlying conceptual bases such as the international style.

"Greening Modernism" references two conditions that are relevant to current global concerns regarding a sustainable future. The first is the existence of a set of fundamental principals and attitudes inherent to the Modern movement as they relate to sustainability. These attitudes apply to all aspects of planning and architecture, from the renovation and upgrading of existing buildings to the design of new ones and the planning of communities and regions. This condition also encompasses a major rationale for the preservation of architecturally and historically relevant buildings as well as providing tools for executing such efforts. The second condition is the need to upgrade the environmental performance of most of the existing building stock, much of which is in the modern style. These two broad areas of endeavor, while presenting very distinct opportunities and challenges, are also closely connected, both in the ways that all building and planning issues are joined through the continuum that is the history of architecture as well as through the existence of the vast inventory of modern-style buildings resulting from the direct misapplication of Modernism. To be clear, most of the buildings that we think of as "modern"—the large-scale anonymous post–World War II structures that populate our cities—have co-opted the name by the application of style at the expense on concept and content. (See 3.1, "Modern-

ism and the Modern Style.") Despite this widespread misunderstanding, the underlying precepts of Modernism remain highly relevant to updating and improving the environmental performance of many modern-style buildings, particularly in that these later buildings possess certain traits in common with the Modern examples whose conceptual bases prompted many of the stylistic gestures that permeate postwar, large-scale architecture. The application of contemporary technologies from a contemporary perspective based on a Modern mindset becomes the foundation for the design of buildings that perform in harmony with nature.

Another aspect of this discussion is its nonlinearity. Just as the architectural process is inherently nonlinear, a building is not designed one component or system at a time, nor does a building magically appear full grown, as did Botticelli's Venus. The process is iterative and often circular. As a design in all of its multi-issue complexity emerges and its issues are more fully understood, early decisions may require revisiting and, perhaps, discarding. Architectural creation does not begin with a clear view to the eventual solution. While one hopes to avoid wasted efforts or explorations of options that lead to obvious dead ends, the design process requires that the architect begin by taking a stand, articulating a thesis. Inherent in this commitment is the acknowledgment that this initial reference point may shift or be abandoned entirely as the true scope and aim of the work become more fully defined.

left
Ciam grid

opposite
AIA Energy Program grid

Yet it is only by making the initial commitment that the process begins. Each subsequent step results in a new set of conditions that produce their own dynamics. Each of these dynamics establishes new benchmarks that not only ground the emerging solutions but also act as bases for the reevaluation of the decisions that have preceded it. As a work of architecture evolves and the number of factors that take part in the dynamic increase, the work takes on a life of its own. The initial commitment becomes subject to reexamination and may, in whole or in part, be jettisoned.

Although a work of architecture is inherently holistic, dependent first and foremost on the synergies of its parts, at any moment the architect is able to work on only a single aspect—a detail, a plan condition, a volumetric study, an elevation, a daylight strategy, an approach to ventilation. Similarly, a book can only address one topic at a time. Yet just as the architect works on each finite aspect in the context of thousands of other conditions, each aspect of this discussion will draw on the entire scope of the subject. Additionally, within the details of each subject, there will be many instances where details of other subjects will add understanding. For example, daylighting is one of the most potent architectural assets and a key element in Modern thought; however, any discussion of daylighting will inevitably involve solar and internal heat gain, thermal mass, thermal conductance, controls, electrical systems, and the First and Second Laws of Thermodynamics.

There have been numerous attempts to organize the entirety of architecture into a unified, coherent presentation. One of the most difficult aspects of any such endeavor is the need to simultaneously show the breadth of the subject without loss of detail and subtlety. A notable example of efforts in this direction was the work of the Congrès Internationaux d'Architecture Moderne (International Congress of Modern Architecture, or CIAM). In 1947, CIAM prepared a matrix intended to define and organize the full scope of the interests of Modern architecture. (See 8.5, "CIAM Grid.") In 1982, the American Institute of Architects used a similar device to organize the content of a professional educational program dealing with the energy performance of buildings. A primary benefit of the matrix approach is that it concisely presents the entire scope of its subject while simultaneously providing convenient cells for the placement of detailed information. Each cell can be developed to whatever level of detail is appropriate without distorting or unbalancing the overall structure of the matrix. With the advent of digital media, new tools are emerging; however, the simultaneous presenting of the broad view and the details has been noticeably rare in computer-based analyses.

Greening Modernism depends on integrated solutions to sets of complex, multipart conditions. The factors will be highly diverse, some quantitative and some qualitative. Their resolution requires intuitive processing and judgment to account for the full range of issues, from scientific and pragmatic to cultural and emotional. This synthesis is architecture.

ENERGY IN ARCHITECTURE PROFESSIONAL DEVELOPMENT PROGRAM

This is an information-base matrix, not a chart of courses or course descriptions. As such, it delineates four levels of information or expertise in each of 16 subject areas.

The first three levels have specific goals against which professionals can measure their own capabilities and qualifications, obtainable through a combination of professional experience, seminars, workshops, and independent study. These goals are not likely to change soon.

The fourth level is intentionally open, since it will undoubtedly develop, grow, and shift in emphasis with the energy field itself—as, indeed, must professionally qualified architects.

		Level 1 A complete overview of energy-conscious design—what it is, why it is necessary, what is involved.	Level 2 Technical skills providing knowledge base to move into full spectrum of energy-conscious design.	Level 3 Comprehensive knowledge and technical skills required to understand and practice energy-conscious design.	Level 4 Detailed knowledge and skills for specialists in specific areas of energy design.
OVERVIEW	The Transition— Historical View	Historical perspective of energy transition generally affecting architecture and urban design.	Detailed knowledge of energy transition specifically affecting architecture and urban design.	Quantifiable data on energy transition specifically affecting architecture and urban planning.	
	Technology and Resource Transition	Overview of technology and resource transitions.	Detailed knowledge of technology and resource transitions.	Quantifiable data on technology and resource transitions.	
	Value Adjustments Transition	Societal transitions.	Detailed knowledge of societal transitions.	Quantifiable data on societal transitions.	
ENERGY ANALYSIS	External Factors	Impact of external factors on energy analysis.	Evaluating external factors in energy analysis.	Using external factors in the design process.	
	Building Envelope	Impact of the building envelope on energy analysis.	Evaluating the building envelope in energy analysis.	Using the building envelope in the design process.	
	Internal Factors	Impact of internal factors on energy analysis.	Evaluating internal factors in energy analysis.	Using internal factors in the design process.	
ENERGY-CONSCIOUS DESIGN	Energy Economics	Economic analysis of energy-conscious measures, government programs encouraging energy-conscious design.	Societal implications of energy economics.	Preparing detailed economic analyses.	
	Energy Regulation	Current energy regulations and rationale for them.	Need for performance standards and solar-rights legislation.	Designing in compliance with energy regulations; simulation of total building performances.	
	Practice and the Design Process	Energy considerations affecting design procedures and office management.	Conceptual or theoretical practice of energy-conscious architecture.	Applying design procedures and office management to energy-conscious design.	
	Energy Use and Program	Program considerations affecting energy usage and consumption in buildings.	Analyzing the impact of program decisions on energy use.	Impact of program decisions on energy use and consumption.	
	Natural Energies	Uses of natural energies in buildings.	Analyzing theoretical use of natural energies, including rules of thumb for various methods and technologies.	Using natural energies in specific building and site applications.	
	Energy Transfer Through the Building Envelope	Aspects of the building envelope affecting energy consumption and capture of natural energies.	Analyzing theoretical impacts of building envelope, including rules of thumb for various methods, building components, and technologies.	Impact of building envelope factors for specific building and site.	
	Thermal Mass	Thermal mass and its impact on energy usage and requirements.	Impact of thermal mass on energy usage patterns of a theoretical building.	Impact of thermal mass on energy usage patterns for specific building and site.	
	Cascading Energies	Cascading energies, including degradation of energy within buildings; cogeneration concepts and community energy systems.	Potential for cascading energy, both natural and nonrenewable; theoretical application of cogeneration.	Evaluating cascading energies and cogeneration, including specific applications and information on technologies and hardware.	
	Building Operation and Control	Need for monitoring buildings.	Automated monitoring systems.	Monitoring techniques, including illustrations of charts and tools used.	
	Dynamic Performance of Buildings	Buildings as dynamic, rather than static, users of energy; impact of this concept on building and system design.	Analyzing and understanding dynamic performance in terms of optimal design.	Analyzing and designing buildings for dynamic performance; basic manual, calculator, and computer techniques.	

Background

1

In the second half of the twentieth century, positions taken by architects became ever more fragmented and ever more divisive. Historic preservation and modern or contemporary design were seen to be at odds with each other, and environmentally responsible architecture was viewed as antithetical to both. Many architects, as well as critics, marketers, and cultural advocates, opted for one or another philosophical camp, resulting in large bodies of work having artificially narrow programmatic, conceptual, and design bases.

1.1

History, or How We Got Here

The compartmentalization of architecture was well suited to discourse based on sound bites and instant communication; however, it undermined the primary imperative of architecture: the synthesis of complex and often contradictory demands into a coherent unity. What emerged was an era of "art" architects, "green" architects, "historic" and "preservation" architects, "interior" architects, "facade" architects, and a multitude of other niche specialists. This fragmentation compromised architecture in two critically important ways. Architects defined the scope of their intentions and the intentions of their work within the sharply narrowed apertures of their specializations. Whether these limits were self-generated or were imposed by the broader cultural context (critics, media, and the like), what resulted was buildings that ignored many of the paramount issues that should have been integral to late-twentieth-century architecture. This is not to say that some works did not succeed brilliantly within the criteria set by their creators; however, they failed as holistic, integral solutions. Given the profound impact that building design and construction have on virtually every aspect of our existence, this failure is not an academic or theoretical

shortcoming. (See chapter 2, "Why Architecture?"). In particular, the unwillingness or inability to consider the interrelationships between making and operating the built environment and the global ecosystem has been a primary component in the problems now facing the natural environment.

The shift in architecture from holism to reductionism corresponded to the emergence of the current environmental crisis. The exact cause-and-effect relationship between these two phenomena may be subject to some question, but there is no doubt that a close connection exists. The products of this distorted architectural practice damaged the environment in that the oversimplification of building design, and the fragmentation of the design process resulted in structures that demand vast amounts of resources, energy and others, and in doing so, place a tremendous burden on the planet. The failure of our society to recognize the severity or, in many cases, even the legitimacy of the environmental crises allowed architects to conduct their work with minimal attention to the potentially catastrophic effects resulting from this work. Much has been written of the failure of modern architec-

ture, that is to say post–World War II architecture, to consider these effects, yet ironically, the sharply narrowed view of architecture was in direct opposition to the principles of the Modern movement of the first half of the twentieth century. Although Modernism emerged in a period when there was little or no awareness of the impending environmental crisis and therefore little direct response to this issue in the early work, a primary tenet of Modernism was the establishment of an architecture that was holistic and integral. (See chapter 3, Modernism, Preservation, and Sustainability.")

The connections between the built and natural environments are now widely understood and accepted. Less broadly accepted but nonetheless critical is the need to solve the pressing problems of shelter and community without sacrificing the elevating effects of culture and art. There is increasing recognition that authenticity of the sense of place, genius loci, is an underlying criterion for measuring success in achieving a viable physical community.

The integration of sustainability, program-driven Modernism, and preservation into a single process appears daunting, yet historically this was the very nature of architecture. Interestingly, the search for a unifying theory runs throughout the Modern movement—not only architecture, but all forms of art, science, and social endeavours. It is not coincidental that Walter Gropius titled the collections of his lectures *The Scope of Total Architecture*, or that the original title of Le Corbusier's watershed book was *Vers une architecture* (literally "towards an architecture," although titled *Towards a New Architecture* in its English translation). The CIAM grid resulted from an ongoing program to organize all of the issues affecting and affected by architecture into a single, useful structure (See 8.5, "CIAM Grid.").

The attitudes and many of the tools that we seek today were well established within Modern architecture. There are new issues that were largely unknown in the 1920s and '30s, yet an understanding of Modernism gives us the framework for organizing a completely contemporary holistic architectural practice. This framework can structure the transformation of modern-style works into high-performance buildings. It offers the understanding of the interrelationships between architectural preservation and sustainable design. It incorporates the tools of contemporary design and construction, which can extend the useful lives of many of our existing buildings, whether historically and culturally significant or simply utilitarian. It also allows us to understand the attitudes which produced the modern-style buildings of the 1950s and '60s in order to more effectively improve their environmental performance and prolong their useful life.

Hong Kong, 1995. Drama occurs
when a rapidly expanding urban
system meets its constraining
boundary.

Since mid-2008, we have seen profound uncertainty regarding the global economy. While the immediate trigger for the crisis was a complex web of opaque relationships involving questionable investment practices, largely involving mortgages, the frenzy of both borrowers and lenders to participate in these highly risky arrangements was driven by an underlying belief that land and buildings would continue to increase in cost, if not in value.

1.2

Recent History

While it may seem ironic in this period of collapsed bubbles and economic dislocation, the premise of the inherent value of real estate is essentially correct. The critical importance and thus the value of resources that are land-area based and therefore finite will continue to increase despite the wild short-term fluctuations in their cost. The limited availability of places to build and materials to build with is an inescapable physical reality. This truth, combined with increasing demand artificially inflated by intense marketing, is classic fuel for speculation. Realities and limitations of the ecosystem compete with economic manipulation to become the basis for planning the built environment. Any vision of the future that relies on expanding consumption of physical resources is inevitably doomed.

Architecture and planning decisions will exert profound influence on virtually all aspects of resource allocation and, as a result, must be integral to any comprehensive approach to an ecologically sound future. Land is a finite resource. In the United States, building construction is the greatest single end-use consumer of many finite resources,

including energy. For example, the construction of a 3,500-square-foot house requires approximately 17,000 gallons of oil, taking into account the manufacture and delivery of building materials and products as well as the energy used on-site. (See 2.2, "The Environmental Impact of Building Construction.") This resource depletion, and the associated environmental degradation, occurs whether or not the house is ever occupied. With rapidly increasing global demand, the cost of these resources, both economic and environmental, will escalate.

The second greatest end-use consumer of energy is infrastructure construction. The reconstruction of our railroads and other mass transit, highways, bridges, and electric generation and distribution systems will compete directly with housing and other building construction regardless of whether a building is essential or discretionary. Further, all construction will be competing with other critical goods and services, such as health care and education.

The essence of this competition—these shortages—was clearly anticipated decades ago.

rapidly renewable materials, such as wood from fast-growing trees which will regenerate in ten or twenty or thirty years; yet we must also recognize that even renewable resources are finite in the rate at which they become available. All of our buildings must be made to deliver their services with the greatest efficiency possible. (See 5.4, "Renewable Resources: Effect on the Environment.")

We must immediately begin the transition to alternative technologies, but these will take many years and vast resources to produce significant benefits. In the interim, conservation offers the greatest potential for immediate impact. However, in seeking sustainability through conservation strategies, it is not realistic to expect a majority to embrace an ascetic lifestyle, nor is this necessary. Rather, we must see that each significant decision incorporates an evaluation of its extended impact and be made accordingly. A recognition that every product consumes some portion of this finite set of resources will lead to a far greater appreciation of those products and to an increase in respect and understanding of the products of previous genera-tions. In the case of buildings and communities, this will reinforce ties to cultural continuity and history that establish a sense of connection to place and time.

One of the underlying guidelines for environmental responsibility has been "reduce, reuse, recycle." The notion of doing more with less has been seen as being at odds with a healthy economy, yet we are

The Limits to Growth, published by the Club of Rome in 1972 and based on broad, interdisciplin-ary research, projected that by the early years of the twenty-first century increasing demand for resources would approach the capacity of the earth to meet those demands. It further anticipated that as we approached these limits, we would experi-ence severe disruptions. Three and a half decades later and having largely ignored the warnings, we are faced with sharply reduced options. The accel-erating rate of global climate change is the result of our approaching the limits of the earth's ability to process our carbon wastes. Domestic price increases for food, as well as global food shortages, trace directly to the growth in the demand for biofu-els. Every shift in the allocation of limited resources will produce secondary effects, most of them undesirable.

There is, however, a concept that can serve as a guide for working through this critical period: sus-tainability. Resources, financial and environmental, must be committed with a view toward both short- and long-term benefits. Every resource that we consume will limit the options available to our chil-dren and their children. We must meet our needs, but we must not squander our children's legacy. We must be smart about our expenditures. For example, we must recycle viable buildings rather than demolish and replace them. When new build-ings are required, we must recognize that precious resources are involved, and we must allocate these resources well. We must, where practical, employ

now seeing that intense marketing efforts to create demands that are far beyond the planet's ability to satisfy, as well as beyond our real needs, have led to conditions that are fundamentally untenable. For architecture, to reduce requires that we meet our legitimate programs with the least expenditure of resources, that we minimize construction. The earth can no longer support vastly overscaled building. Efficient programming and planning, one of the traditional services provided by architects, can make it possible to meet human and social goals with greatly lessened environmental degradation.

Reusing entails extending the life of our existing building stock. This may involve historic or landmark building preservation or the performance upgrade of utilitarian, background structures that, although essentially sound, consume resources wastefully or are inefficient in meeting current program needs. Contemporary technologies, particularly those involving information management and control systems, make possible significant performance improvements with very little impact on building space or configuration.

Recycling may be seen in two ways. From an environmental perspective, the most desirable is adaptive reuse, that is, the transformation of an entire building from one use to another. When physical components of our building stock are reused in place, the environmental impacts that result from resource extraction, processing, and transformation are dramatically reduced. Building materials may also be recycled in the more commonly used sense of collecting and reprocessing the debris from demolition. The benefits of this approach are far smaller than from adaptive reuse and, in some cases, may be nonexistent, as when more environmental damage is done in the reprocessing than would have occurred if new material had been used. (See 4.5, "Energy Quality: The Second Law of Thermodynamics.")

Throughout this period of upheaval, there has been a tendency to equate reduced resource usage with a reduction in quality of life. While the effects of limited resources will certainly impact the ways in which carry on our lives, they should also cause us to reconsider how we value experiences, particularly those that require resource expenditure. It is a commonplace that people who have close encounters with death savor life with particular intensity. Assuming that we are able to achieve sufficient levels of sustainability that human existence survives and flourishes, our appreciation for authentic experience should be enhanced by the understanding that these experiences, along with physical resources, are finite. This realization offers an elevated quality of life decoupled from what has been the unabated devouring of our planet.

2

Why Architecture?

More than any other discipline, architecture and planning directly affect humankind's impact on the natural environment, for better or for worse. Our buildings consume resources and create pollution in their construction and demolition as well as in their operation. Decisions on building placement, configuration, and density will profoundly influence the need for infrastructure construction, from highways and mass transit to water, sewer, and power systems. Infrastructure use patterns create their own set of demands on the ecosystem.

2.1

The Measure of Architecture

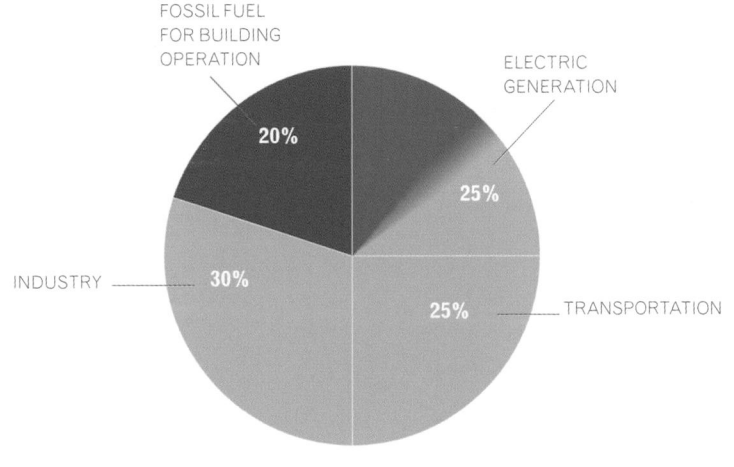

PRIMARY CONSUMERS OF ENERGY RESOURCES IN THE UNITED STATES

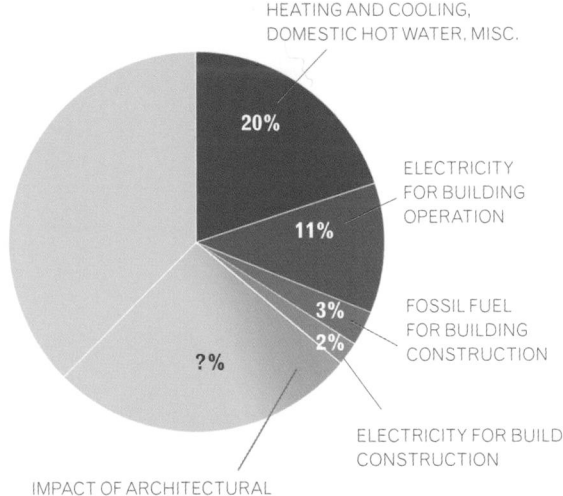

U.S. ENERGY AFFECTED BY ARCHITECTURAL AND PLANNING DECISIONS

Architecture directly affects more than 40 percent of all energy consumed in the United States. Building operation—heating, cooling, lighting, pumps, elevators, and such—requires nearly one third of all energy used. (See 2.4, "The Impact of Building Upgrade: Operating Savings.")

Building construction takes another 5 percent. Infrastructure construction—roads and highways, water and sewage systems, power generation and distribution—use about 4 percent. Granted, systems are not generally the direct responsibility of architects, but their size and extent will be heavily influenced by architectural and planning decisions. (See 4.2, "Embodied Energy.")

There is a new, global awareness of the finite nature of critical resources, and architects must redefine the measure of what they produce. Traditionally, building performance has been measured against size, typically floor area. This has been the basis for determining and describing efficiency. It is not, however, a meaningful approach to the

top
Breakdown of energy use in the U.S. by major categories.

bottom
Portions of U.S. energy use affected by architectural decisions. Note that some portion of Transportation is impacted.

above
Stillman House I (1950).

opposite
Stillman House II (1965).

overleaf
Stillman House III (1974).
Marcel Breuer and Associates
(MBA/GPS).

The three houses, although separated by twenty-four years, share the commitment to provide houses that, while meticulously designed, do not overwhelm the understanding and appreciation of context and the essential activities of human life.

creation of a sustainable built environment, which must be dependent first and foremost on weighing the resources consumed and environmental damage caused against the quantity and quality of service and utility. We can double the fuel efficiency of our cars, but this will be negated if we create living patterns that double the need for automobile use. Similarly, we can improve the environmental performance of our buildings in terms of energy use per square foot, but this benefit will be lost if we construct more buildings than we need to enjoy rich and fulfilled lives. In order for building design and regional planning to proceed rationally, it is necessary to understand the issues and their interconnections, both in behavior and magnitude. We must also understand what is necessary to live well.

Rufus Stillman, a longtime friend and client of Marcel Breuer, recalled that in the early 1950s, over a chess board and a glass of wine, Breuer had said to him that "we may not have a lot of money but we know how to live well." Stillman went on to say that in a similar setting in 1980, when both men had achieved a substantial degree of success, Breuer commented, "Rufus, we may have a lot of money, but we know how to live well." Quality of life ought not be dependent on either money or resource consumption.

Still, architects are not, or at least should not, be primarily concerned with measuring energy delivered to their buildings or with the primary resources required to deliver that energy, but rather in providing built spaces—interior and exterior—in which people can conduct the activities of their lives. As such, the measure of the efficiency of a work of architecture is ultimately how well the resources have been used to satisfy human needs, whether pragmatic, cultural, or spiritual. A small building may embody more energy per square foot than a larger one. It may also use more operating energy per square foot. However, if the smaller building is fully able to provide the same services with less total embodied energy and less operating energy, it becomes the more efficient solution. Building costs may be defined in many units, including those of money, energy, resources, or carbon or other pollutants; however, rather than measuring cost per square foot, the basis for determining the performance of architecture must the comparison of cost against the overall quality of life provided—a new paradigm.

Infrastructure construction,
Le Pont de Normandie, Le Havre, France.

Construction activity, the creation of our buildings and infrastructure, consumes approximately 10 percent of all energy used in the United States. Building construction alone consumes more than 5 percent of the national total. This is in addition to energy required for operation once the buildings are complete.

2.2

The Environmental Impact of Building Construction

Before dealing with specific numbers, it should be pointed out that if this were primarily a technical treatise, virtually all of the data used here would be subject to extensive qualifications. While sources disagree on exact figures, there is good correlation among the various studies on the impact of construction, particularly as it involves energy use. As such, this information is important not only to understand the quantitative data, it is also essential to address the underlying concepts—the very basis for the consideration of sustainability.

For quantitative purposes, there are strong connections between energy use and sustainability. Data on energy use are widely available and verifiable and the units that quantify energy are commonly understood and interchangeable. For most of the quantitative discussions, I will use energy consumption as the measure of performance. (See 4.1, "Energy: A Measure of Sustainability.")

Essential to the discussions of resource consumption is whether they refer to source (primary) use or end use. The difference between the two measures may be one of degree or of magnitude. For example,

for each one hundred gallons of oil consumed at a building, it takes approximately ten additional gallons of oil (or their equivalent in other forms of energy) to drill, transport, refine, transport the primary resource, in this case crude oil. In other words, every gallon of oil consumed at a building actually demands about 1.1 gallons of source energy. (See 5.2, "End-Use versus Source.")

If, however, we look instead at a kilowatt-hour of electricity consumed at a building, the effects are quite different. A modern fossil-fuel generating plant will operate at about 40 percent efficiency. This efficiency is limited by the Second Law of Thermodynamics, which states that although the total quantity of energy in a closed system will remain constant, the quality of energy will tend to degrade to the level of its surroundings. Conversely, in order to raise the quality of energy, an additional quantity of energy must be introduced. Electricity is high-quality energy. (See 4.5, "Energy Quality: The Second Law of Thermodynamics.")

In other words, in order to produce one unit of electricity, it is necessary to commit two and one-half

units of fuel at the generator. But this is not the end. The energy has to be transformed, transported, and transformed again before it arrives at the building's meter. The net result is an overall efficiency of about 30 percent, meaning that each unit of electrical energy delivered to a building has required about three and one-third units of fuel at the generator. This still does not get to the total source energy required to create and deliver that one unit of electricity. Getting the fuel to the generator requires energy for extraction, processing and transportation. The result is that each unit of electric energy delivered to a building will require the input of nearly four units of source energy.

The cost of a particular form of a resource is indicative of its quality. Compare, for example, electricity and crude oil, the first being a very high level of energy and the second a basic raw material. A kilowatt-hour is the equivalent of 3,412 Btu. A gallon of #6 oil will produce about 144,000 Btu of heat. It would take about 42 kilowatt-hours to provide heat equivalent to burning one gallon of oil. The present cost of a kilowatt-hour of electricity is about $0.16, or about $6.75 for the heat equivalent in a gallon of oil. The price of #6 oil in mid-2010 was about $2.50 per gallon. The high price of electricity is due to the energy that must be added and the equipment—generators, transformers, and transmission lines—necessary to produce and deliver the energy in its final form. All of these have environmental costs.

A similar condition exists for construction. The value—economic, societal, or environmental—of the materials that make up a building, a road, a power station, or any other built work is primarily due to the resources needed to raise the level of those materials, rather than the resource value of the materials themselves. The environmental cost of construction is less the result of the resources used directly by the construction industry than of all of supporting activities that occur beyond the perimeter of the building site. These indirect expenditures are nonreversible. If a building is demolished, the materials will retain their own intrinsic value; however, all of the input that raised their levels and organized them into the new complex entity that is the building will be lost.

Overall, the environmental value of salvaging the materials that make up the structures that result from the construction industries represent about one-tenth the total direct and indirect input needed to create the buildings in the first place. This will be offset in part or entirely by the environmental cost of the demolition process itself. While there is certainly a reason to recycle building materials when demolition can not be avoided, their value is in no way equivalent to that of the building they once formed.

The environmental impact of building construction results primarily from the indirect costs, all of the processes and activities that transform raw materials into a finished built object.

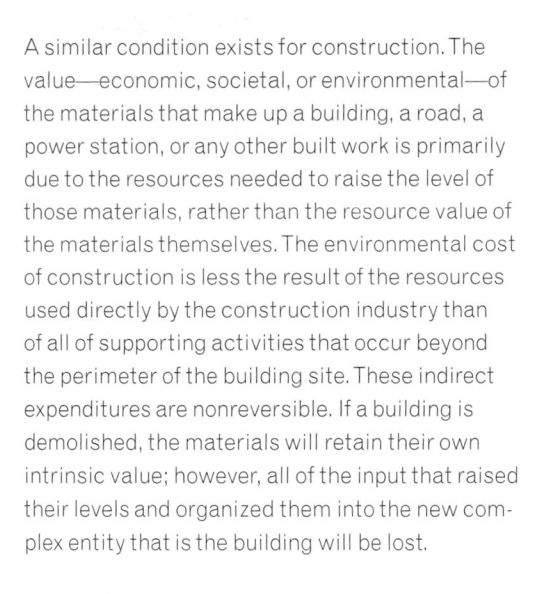

oppposite
Throughout the U.S., nineteenth-century buildings continue to meet needs while contributing to the physical and cultural continuity.

A program to upgrade and reuse existing buildings instead of demolishing and replacing them can produce savings in the construction process alone equivalent to nearly 4 billion gallons of oil per year.

This is the equivalent of removing about 10 million cars from the road.

2.3

The Impact of Building Upgrade: Embodied Resources

Based on considerations of sustainability, why take the trouble to green the inventory of existing buildings, whether Modern, modern style, or historicist? The reasons are found in the environmental effects of the construction process itself and from building operation. As noted previously, the use of energy as the metric for environmental performance is in large part based on the close tracking between energy use and other key markers, such as emissions of greenhouse gases and other pollutants. It is also because large amounts of data are readily available.

For every square foot of new building, the construction process requires the energy equivalent of between five and fifteen gallons of oil. This is the energy required to extract the raw materials needed for construction, to transport these materials to processing facilities, to transport the processed materials to the factories where building components are produced, to manufacture those components, to transport the components to the building sites, and to assemble the components. It includes the energy used at the building site itself and the energy used at the many offices where the

building design and construction administration are carried out. This is the embodied energy of construction.

While it is relatively simple to quantify the energy that was required to construct any particular building, this is not the basis for determining its environmental value going forward. Environmental value must be based on the avoided damages—the energy savings or savings in other environmental criteria that will result from the reuse of a building or building components *compared with* its replacement with new construction providing similar service. The resources used for the creation of a building have already been committed, and taking advantage of the value and utility that resulted from this expenditure will avoid additional expenditure. (See 4.3, "A Handbook of Embodied Energy in Building Construction.")

The comprehensive upgrading of existing buildings will, in itself, require the commitment—the embodiment—of considerable energy, but, a conservative analysis shows that even with comprehensive upgrades, the reuse of existing structures will

save at least one third, and probably one half, of the energy that would be required for new construction. In other words, depending on the type of building being replaced and the amount of reconstruction required to bring that building up to high performance standards, each square foot of renovated building will save the equivalent of anywhere from 300,000 to 1,200,000 Btu, the equivalent of two to eight gallons of oil, compared with replacing it with new construction.

A building-specific case study offers an example of the order of magnitude of the potential savings in embodied energy realized when reusing an existing building. In 2006, Cayuga County purchased a site in downtown Cleveland that included a 280,000-square-foot office building. The twenty-nine-story tower was completed in 1971 as the headquarters of a large bank but had been vacant for a number of years. The plan was to demolish the tower and build a new county office building. While similar situations are constantly occurring, a unique aspect of this case was that the tower was the one high-rise building in the United States designed by Marcel Breuer. As a result, a number of diverse interest groups joined in a campaign to preserve the building. (See 9.1, "Embodied Energy in the Cleveland Trust Tower.")

The embodied energy saved by reusing the building, compared with what would have been embodied in a new building, was equivalent to about 1.7 million gallons of oil, six gallons per square foot. While the case study was based on total replacement of all mechanical and electrical systems, all glazing and window systems, and virtually all interior finishes, the savings are still on the high side of the generalized estimates, and the cultural benefits of saving the work of this renowned Modern architect go far beyond the environmental effects. They reinforce our cultural heritage. Yet this last consideration dramatizes one of the great problems facing environmentally driven building reuse. Very few works of architecture receive a level of acclaim that draws people to their defense. Without this acclaim, thoughtless demolition and associated environmental damage is occurring daily.

One scenario for considering the nationwide energy savings associated with re-use is to identify the quantity of viable but dated buildings that currently exist in the United States, and then evaluate the overall effect of greening these buildings, compared to demolishing and replacing them. While there are no readily available data on the percentage of the existing building stock targeted for demolition and replacement, it is possible to develop some broad projections based on informed assumptions. For example, approximately 160 million square feet of new office building is constructed in the US each year. If half of this office space (80 million square feet) were provided by the reuse of existing building stock upgraded to current high-performance standards and using innovating space planning, savings in embodied energy would be approximately 50 trillion Btu, the equivalent of 350 million gallons of oil, when compared with demolishing and replacing these buildings. The construction quantity is an annual figure, so these savings could be repeated at least until the current poorly performing and underutilized building stock was renovated to high-performance standards.

In addition to the savings in energy and other resources, the reuse of existing buildings also reduces the burden on landfill and other disposal facilities, whose total capacity is also finite. (See 5.6, "Waste Management.")

oppposite
Patterns of embodied energy input to 18 new building construction types from *The Handbook of Energy Use for Building Construction* (1981).

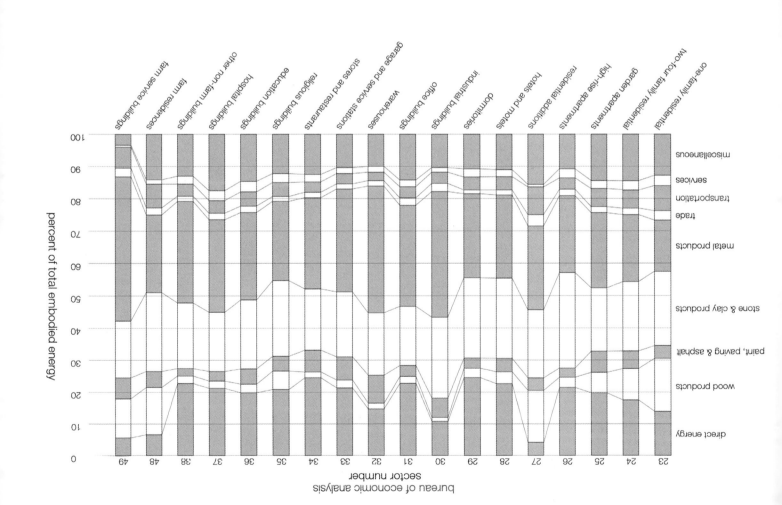

The energy required to operate buildings in the United States is approximately one third of the total national energy use. A program to upgrade older buildings to current standards can lower United States energy use by the equivalent of nearly 2 billion gallons of oil each year. At the end of a ten-year program, cumulative annual operating energy savings would be equal to the effect of about 100 billion gallons of oil, the equivalent of removing about 30 million cars from the roads for that entire ten-year period.

2.4

The Impact of Building Upgrade: Operating Savings

The benefits of building or rebuilding to high-performance levels can also be quantified. While there is a wide range of energy usage among 1950s and '60s office buildings, a representative case offers some insight as to the potential savings. Typical energy use per square foot for a midcentury suburban low-rise structure in the northeast United States would be in the range of 150,000–250,000 Btu per square foot. This would include the energy for lighting, heating, cooling and ventilation, and miscellaneous pumps and motors. A similar building designed to comply with current energy codes will use 85,000–100,000 Btu per square foot, while a high-performance building will operate at 50,000–55,000 Btu per square foot.

The energy figures listed above represent the usage at the building itself. The numbers for source energy, the energy required to generate electricity and process the oil and gas delivered to the building, are 400,000–600,000 Btu per square foot for the 1960s building, 250,000–300,000 Btu per square foot for the contemporary code-compliant building, and 130,000–150,000 Btu per square foot for the high-performance building. (See 5.2, "End Use versus Source.")

It is important to note that the high-performance figures are based on a building design that measures only added costs that would be recovered from energy savings in less than three years without relying on subsidies. In fact, because of trade-offs between the increased cost for higher performance components and equipment, and the savings from smaller and more compact systems, the total cost of a high-performance building will be comparable to a conventional building.

Upgrades of existing office buildings can be expected to produce savings in source energy for building operation of 250,000–450,000 Btu per square foot per year. If this were applied to the 80 million square feet of converted building described earlier, there would be savings of about 24 trillion Btu per year, in addition to the 50 trillion Btu in embodied energy savings described in 2.3. However, unlike the savings resulting from the reduction of embodied energy, operating upgrades continue

ENERGY SAVINGS IN BTU X 10¹² (TRILLION BTU OR 1,000,000,000,000 BTU)

YEAR	Embodied energy savings achieved this year (trillion Btu)	Annual operating energy savings achieved this year (trillion Btu)	Annual operating energy savings cumulative (trillion Btu)	Current annual savings for this year (trillion Btu)	Cummulative savings total (trillion Btu)
1	50	24	2	2	74
2	50	24	48	48	172
3	50	24	72	72	294
4	50	24	96	96	440
5	50	24	120	120	610
6	50	24	144	144	804
7	50	24	168	168	1,022
8	50	24	192	192	1.264
9	50	24	216	216	1,530
10	50	24	240	240	1,820

ENERGY SAVINGS IN GALLONS OF OIL X 10⁹ (BILLION GAL OR 1,000,000,000 GAL)

YEAR	Embodied energy savings achieved this year (billion gallons of oil)	Annual operating energy savings achieved this year (billion gallons of oil)	Annual operating energy savings cumulative (billion gallons of oil)	Current annual savings for this year (billion gallons of oil)	Cummulative savings total (billion gallons of oil)
1	0.35	0.17	0.17	0.52	0.52
2	0.35	0.17	0.34	0.69	1.21
3	0.35	0.17	051	0.86	2.07
4	0.35	0.17	0.68	1.03	3.10
5	0.35	0.17	0.85	1.20	4.30
6	0.35	0.17	1.02	1.37	5.67
7	0.35	0.17	1.19	1.54	7.21
8	0.35	0.17	1.36	1.71	8.92
9	0.35	0.17	1.53	1.88	10.80
10	0.35	0.17	1.70	2.05	12.85

to produce savings throughout the life of the building. In a multiyear evaluation, annual operations savings are cumulative.

Looking at the combined savings in embodied and operating energies, a nationwide, comprehensive ten-year program applied just to office building construction would save a total of nearly 2 quadrillion Btu, the equivalent of almost 13 billion gallons of oil.

So far, consideration has been limited to office buildings, annually constructed at the rate of about 160 million square feet per year. Total US building construction is approximately 3.7 billion square feet per year, about 23 times that of office building alone. Assuming that the average savings per square foot for the total are only one third those possible for office buildings, a ten-year program for building reuse and upgrade offers potential energy savings equivalent to about 100 billion gallons of oil.

As a point of reference, the Energy Information Administration of the U.S. Department of Energy projections for recoverable oil from the Arctic National Wildlife Refuge (ANWR) are 5.1 billion barrels (214 billion gallons) with 95 percent certainty and 10.2 billion barrels (428 billion gallons) as likely recoverable. In other words, a national ten-year program for building upgrade and reuse would produce savings equal to one quarter to one half of the entire projected potential of ANWR. Further, allowing for an additional two-year period

for design and initial implementation, this program would have achieved these savings twelve years after commencing, the time ANWR could produce its first useful product. Those operating energy savings would of course continue well beyond the twelve-year point.

Obviously, in terms of embodied energy, the optimal approach would be to use the buildings as they currently exist. This has several drawbacks. First, most of these buildings require much more energy to operate than do contemporary, high-performance structures. Second, many of these buildings do not meet their programmatic challenges particularly effectively or efficiently—they do not provide the best workplaces, nor do they make best use of their available spaces. These buildings are at or rapidly approaching an age of fifty years, however, as is noted in the Cleveland Trust analysis (see 2.3), even after a comprehensive upgrade, in many cases including the replacement of the building skin, the savings in embodied energy are tremendous.

As a society, we have a history of casually discarding buildings and replacing them. Recognizing the need to bring consumption under control, it is clear that we must begin a serious program of extending the useful life of our inventory of built resources.

Energy savings from a ten-year program to reuse and upgrade office buildings in the U.S.

An analytic Modernist approach to issues of planning and architecture that recognizes the absolute limits of resource availability will lead to solutions that incorporate environmental responsibility as a primary design imperative. This, integrated into comprehensive solutions that recognize the pragmatic, cultural, and spiritual goals of architecture, will produce true sustainability.

2.5

What's Green about Modern?

To understand the essential relationships between Modernism and sustainability, it is first necessary to be clear as to what is meant by each word. The phrase Modern architecture is perhaps the most misunderstood and misused expression in the parlance of the architect's profession. There are any number of reasons why this is so and, in seeking to deal constructively with Modernism and sustainability, it is helpful to place the issues into context.

The concept of "international style" or "modern style" was consciously created, in large part, as a set of limitations to facilitate discussion and criticism of what was, in fact, the highly complex and varied set of ideas and work that were Modern architecture (See 3.1, "Modernism and the Modern Style.") In fact, architects and planners working under the Modern banner would have been appalled at the notion that their work was connected by style rather than philosophy, approach, and methodology; writings of Le Corbusier and Walter Gropius make this explicitly clear. (See 3.2, "Modernism, the Modern Style, and Post modernism.")

The work of the Modern movement was directed toward defining essential problems, identifying the resources—physical, intellectual, and cultural—that could be brought to bear, analyzing optimal strategies for applying the resources, and designing solutions based on the analyses. With the understanding that we are experiencing an environmental crisis that could endanger our survival, new critical criteria have emerged. Key among these is the realization that all physical resources are finite, and any strategy predicated on expanding consumption will fail. Modernism of the early twenty-first century will not look like Modernism of the early or mid-twentieth century, but it will evolve from a similar process.

In simplest terms, to act sustainably means to consider how each decision will affect future generations and to set as a goal having these effects be beneficial rather than damaging. While there is no way to fully anticipate the results of any actions, general trends can be influenced to favor one outcome over another. Recognizing that many of our most vital resources are finite and that we are approaching the absolute limits to their avail-

ability, it is clear that to continue consuming these resources in the hope that some as yet theoretical technology will solve the problem, leaving the denouement to our children and grandchildren, is not sustainable.

Given the rapid changes in both technologies and environmental conditions, the traditional goal of looking seven generations ahead, however laudable, seems unrealistic. It is virtually certain that the next hundred years will see the development of technologies that are currently unimaginable. It is also unmistakably clear that human activity is causing profound and potentially irreversible environmental changes that can be seen within the time frame of a single generation. The demand for action is immediate, however; the results of current planning and architectural work will affect the global ecology for many decades to come. We are charged with creating context-specific designs despite the fact that the resulting buildings and communities will be functioning in future contexts which we cannot foresee. Whereas Modernism of the early twentieth century was marked by a sense of certainty of the endurance of solutions, Modernism in the early twenty-first century must address an unknowable future. Still, general possibilities can be projected and Modernist thought encompasses the methodologies to accommodate those possibilities, supporting solutions that have long-term green benefits. Ironically, a modern style approach or, for that matter, any approach that is driven by an a priori commitment to any particular

style is diametrically opposed to green planning, and is environmentally counterproductive.

Modernism, with its insistence on the making of architecture that is holistically responsive to multiple and complex influences, influences that themselves behave holistically, does not lend itself to simplistic reductionism, to definition by sound bite. Difficulties in addressing this essential complexity encouraged efforts to compartmentalize and oversimplify the movement in order to facilitate popular discussion and marketing. Architecture was defined in terms of tableaux and stylistic gestures that, in turn, promoted superficial presentation and understanding. This does not, however, accommodate work that achieves much of its meaning through the integrated resolution of multiple, complex issues.

The problem is compounded by the very business of architecture: most of the marketing occurs in brief presentations and public relations campaigns largely built on two- or three-paragraph reviews. This, coupled with the inevitable trend toward critics and "historians" whose work is tailored to an audience that expects a reductivist product, has all but eliminated comprehensive discussion of architecture, at least in the popular media.

By definition, if the success of a work of architecture is based on its integrated resolution of all relevant issues—on its holistic qualities—the effects of narrowing the scope of these issues will reduce

or distort these considerations. While this applies to any overall view of architecture, nowhere is the destructive effect of reductionism more apparent than in the relationship between architecture and sustainability. The practice of truly sustainable architecture is no more about the unconsidered application of the latest green electronics or whirligigs than the practice of Modern architecture was about the thoughtless use of elements such as ribbon windows or the free plan. In both cases, certain features tend to recur because, on careful consideration, they make sense for the particular project. The mistake, however, is in viewing any work that incorporates these elements as being de facto sustainable or Modern.

There is a tendency to think of appropriate design strategies for sustainability as being about getting along with less and, as a result, suggesting a reduced quality of life. Design based on avoidance of wasteful or extravagant use of resources is characterized as minimalist. Neither is the case. What we have experienced during the past several decades is a society in which the apparently easy access to material goods and resources has so devalued experience that it has become difficult to differentiate between authentic and artificial. The need to be selective in our choices forces the setting of priorities and, as such, a greater appreciation of the selections made. Selective planning and design will highlight authentic experience that will, in turn, encourage far greater care of the resources, both natural and cultural, necessary for such experiences to happen.

3

Modernism, Preservation, and Sustainability

The Modern movement in architecture, generally associated with European practice in the first half of the twentieth century, was based largely on a commitment to create works that were shaped by a series of significant issues that could be articulated and addressed. Those issues ranged from the pragmatic—space programming, structure, construction—to the sublime—cultural innovation, spiritual enhancement. Although intensely rigorous, this work was by definition antidogmatic.

The development of the concept of "modern style" or "international style," whether through intention or misunderstanding, was fundamentally antithetical to Modernism. The rejection of the a priori application of style, whether neoclassical or gridded curtain wall, was, and remains, at the heart of a true Modernist attitude.

3.1

Modernism and the Modern Style

Modernism in architecture generally references a portion of the work of the first half of the twentieth century; however, like all significant cultural, scientific, and technological movements, it has its beginnings well in advance of its recognized start date, and its effects are still strongly felt. The seeds of Modernism might be found in the industrial revolution of the early nineteenth century and the industrialized production that became prevalent by the mid-nineteenth century. Certainly, such Modern forerunners as the Crystal Palace or the Eiffel Tower could not have occurred were it not for factory production.

Modernism might be seen as growing out of the reconsideration of the visual arts brought about by the advent of photography and the work of Cézanne, Monet, and Seurat in the final quarter of the nineteenth century. The idea that a work of art might be based on a conceptual view of itself—abstraction—has an important place in the evolution of a Modern architecture in that in itself, the process of analyzing, designing, and realizing a building might be the basis for that building's appearance, rather than the application of some preconceived style.

Modern architecture could not have happened without the availability of concentrated energy, primarily petroleum. The Drake oil well, which is usually cited as the first commercial operation of its kind, was drilled in 1859 and began the pattern of exponential growth in hydrocarbon fuel consumption that now so threatens the ecosystem. Here is one of the great ironies in the history of architecture and environmental consciousness: the technologies that underlie the evolution of Modern thought were dependent on readily available energy sources—electricity, oil, and gas. The modern city, with all of its global environmental benefits, is a product of Modernism. (See 8.8, "Cities, Energy, and Architecture.")

The same easy access to vast energy resources essential to Modern architecture also made the modern style possible, and in doing so created the false belief that architects could do whatever they pleased, that the application of energy would address all questions of the interior environments thus created. While this approach once seemed viable, it has become increasingly apparent that it is not sustainable.

In order to appropriately apply the lessons of Modern architecture to sustainable design, it is essential to differentiate between *Modernism and the modern style*. While there are certainly characteristics common among Modern works, they vary widely in appearance. Consider, for example, such iconic houses as Villa Savoye, Fallingwater, and Farnsworth House. Each is the work of a recognized Modern master—Le Corbusier, Frank Lloyd Wright, and Ludwig Mies van der Rohe—yet each has a distinct style. Each appears very different from the others.

Consider also the remarkable variation among Modern museums such as the Guggenheim by Wright, the Whitney of Marcel Breuer, Josep Lluís Sert's Fondation Maeght, or Le Corbusier's Tokyo museum. There is no singular style that may be drawn from Le Corbusier's Chapel at Ronchamp, Wright's Unity Temple, Breuer's St. Johns Abbey Church, or Saarinen's chapel at MIT, all Modern churches. Modern architecture has no particular preconceived appearance or immediately recognizable but, rather, is driven by the complex set of conditions of context—physical, cultural, programmatic—for each individual commission.

The specificity of design, including but in no way limited to appearance, in response to each unique condition and application, is an inherent quality of Modern work. The appropriateness of each approach provides both the basis for a visual solution that conveys information about the forces that

shaped the design, and a building that interacts positively and synergistically with its surroundings—built and natural.

The analytical rigor required by Modernism is key to the innovation, variation, and richness of the resulting buildings, but it is also highly problematic to powerful sectors within architecture and the broader realms of culture. It is difficult to discuss Modernism or Modern building in a few choice words or phrases. It is not receptive to sound bites. Critics and journalists cannot effectively discuss Modernist work with a few catchwords, nor can they force individual works into preconceived descriptive cubbyholes. Equally to the point, architectural marketers have great difficulty presenting firms' works and approaches using neat packages that can be conveyed to prospective clients in a fifteen-minute presentation or a short brochure. Modernism is highly resistant to branding.

In 1932, Henry-Russell Hitchcock and Philip Johnson either coined or popularized the term *international style* for a show of Modernist work at the Museum of Modern Art in New York City. Whether by chance or by intention, this became the starting point for the dilution and eventually almost total misunderstanding of the precepts of Modern architecture. In fact, Modernism argued forcefully against an academy of style. One need only look at the works of the architects who participated in CIAM. (See 8.5 "CIAM Grid.") The very establishment of CIAM demonstrates the effort

to identify and clarify common ground among a number of very different architects. Further, those who participated in CIAM represented only a small, albeit important, percentage of Modern architects. Rather than a style or a school, Modernism was and is a methodology and an attitude that draws on a vast complex of conditions for its creations. Essential to Modernism is the eschewal of reliance on formulaic, doctrinaire strategies. However, the emergence of the phrase *modern style* became the basis for the misappropriation of the words *Modern and Modernism* by those who would use "modern" as a brand without substance.

Perhaps even more problematic than the general misconception of the Modern process was the claim that Modernism somehow justified the modern style, which in turn validated the creation of vast quantities of repetitive, unresponsive buildings throughout the country. The ability to reproduce very large buildings with minimal innovation or recognition of the specifics of place, climate, culture, and history greatly reduced the time and effort required within architectural offices, making these projects increasingly profitable. It also produced buildings that were remarkably destructive to the environment.

The failure, in environmental terms, of the great majority of modern style buildings is the result of a convergence of factors. The ability to design and construct buildings with little attention to geography and climate was only possible because of the availability of mechanical and electrical systems that could overcome the inherent deficiencies in the basic design of the building itself. We see essentially the same modern style buildings in New York, Dallas, Pittsburgh, and Atlanta. The intensity of the use of these mechanical and electrical systems was supported by the artificially low cost of energy. The overall approach was well suited to both large-scale architectural practice and cultural journalism. This convergence created a number of unfortunate conditions. First, it led to a pervasive attitude that there was, essentially, an environmental discontinuity at the skin of the building. That is, the interior environment was treated as being totally separate from the exterior environment. Regardless of what was happening outside the building, the interior environment was created by mechanical and electrical systems, totally dependent on energy resources for their operation.

Not only did the design of these buildings ignore the potential benefits that could be derived from the exterior environment, as can immediately be seen when electric lights are in operation at the perimeter of a glass-skinned building in the middle of the day, their design compounded the problem by requiring energy-consuming systems to neutralize the effects of the exterior environment, effects that could have been largely controlled by the building envelope. Such design has obvious sustainability issues, and it compromised the quality of the interior spaces that were created, both in quantifiable and emotional terms. Further, the uniformity of the

resulting buildings produces a homogeneity that destroys historical and cultural regionalism and sense of place.

The shift from Modernism, with its insistence on project-specific analysis and synthesis, to the modern style, with its highly generalized application of motifs, was a self-reinforcing process that rapidly transformed the greater part of mid-twentieth-century architecture in the United States. Architects were able to reduce staff time required to design and manage very large scale projects, thus increasing profitability. Critics and journalists were able to discuss these projects by focusing only on the superficial differences. Clients and the public at large came to view the work of architects as being primarily the creation of these superficial differences. Architects were able to market their work based on these differences—the emergence of "signature style."

The availability of energy resources and the advances in technologies to harness them permitted the abandonment of climatologically responsive building design. Lost were the innovative designs that maximize the use of daylight, gravity, and prevailing wind ventilation, direct solar heat gain, and thermal mass to temper diurnal swings that are seen in buildings whose time or place did not offer the option of creating comfortable interior environments by the application of mechanical and electrical systems. Lost was architecture that not only offered human comfort at minimum environmental

cost but also established regional characteristics. This sense of place, genius loci resulting from environmentally responsive building and planning, is both emotionally and intellectually satisfying. Its creation becomes an essential programmatic criterion for contemporary Modern work.

It is ironic that the technological and scientific advances that made Modern architecture possible also allowed the development of the shortsighted modern style and seduced the culture into its acceptance.

By the mid-1960s, many of the deficiencies of the modern style had become apparent. Unfortunately, we had become so conditioned to considering architecture as style that most of the proposed corrections merely substituted one style for another. This in no way addressed the loss of the Modern process that plagued the modern style. In fact, those who sought to elevate the importance of this stylistic battle made a conscious effort to conflate Modernism and the modern style, claiming that the new styles were fundamental challenges to the Modern movement. Nothing could have been farther from the truth.

Although the modern style essentially turned its back on the Modern design process, the design process can reform the massive inventory of modern style buildings for environmental responsiveness. Modernism will green the modern style.

Near Leadville, Colorado. The essential elements of Modern rationalism are incorporated in the volumetric simplicity of the house, its symmetrical entry, fenestration, dormer, and pyramidal roof, all accentuated by the regular but asymmetric porch which mitigates the harsh west sun— rigorous geometry responding to natural phenomena.

The following was written in 1976 in response to an article by Ada Louise Huxtable, a critic whose work I have always greatly admired. A significantly shortened version was published by the *New York Times*. After more than thirty years, while I find some of my observations somewhat oversimplified, two overriding points still seem accurate and relevant. First, despite great advances in both design and construction technologies since the end of World War II, most architectural discussion has focused on issues of style and these issues have had relatively little to do with addressing global sustainability. Second, the tenets of Modernism remain the basis for a contemporary architecture that can support the advancement of global sustainability.

3.2

Modernism, the Modern Style, and Postmodernism

The article by Huxtable in the *New York Times* of June 27, 1976, raises a very serious question regarding the future of architecture. In the opening paragraph she writes:

Modern architecture is at a turning point. A half century after the revolution that ushered in the modern movement and changed the look and character of the built world, we are in the midst of a counter revolution.

She goes on to cite the influence of Mies van der Rohe and Le Corbusier, and closes the paragraph saying, "The theory and practice of modernism are under serious attack."

The article suggests that a group of architectural "young Turks" represented by Robert Venturi and Denise Scott Brown have mounted a challenge to the fundamental concepts of "Modernism" generated in Europe in the 1920s. In fact, this new "movement" neither challenges nor comes to grips with the basic concerns raised at that time. Modern architecture is indeed at a turning point, but the alternatives are not represented by Venturi on the

the statements of the Moderns themselves with those principles that today's critics have attributed to them and that they then attack.

Early in her article, Ms. Huxtable writes, "The gospel according to Gideon and Gropius," and by implication the gospel of the Modern movement, "preached . . . rejection of the past." Later in the article she describes architecture as " . . . one profession that went through the 'history is irrelevant' bit half a century ago."

In 1939, Walter Gropius, talking about architectural education, indicated the importance he saw in the study of history.

one hand and van der Rohe on the other, but rather by a choice between architecture of style and architecture of reason.

As a basis for their attack, the "New" movement of the 1970s ascribes concepts to the Moderns of the '20s that, in some cases, are exactly the concepts that the Modern movement sought to overcome. Straw men are raised and then knocked over by the "young Turks" who claim to be challenging the very foundations of Modernism. Bearing in mind that there have been considerable changes in the environment in which buildings are created between the '20s and today, it is worth exploring

Studies in the history of art and architecture, intellectual and analytical in character, make the student familiar with the conditions and reasons which have brought about the visual expression of the different periods; i.e., the changes in philosophy, in politics, and in the means of production caused by new inventions.

In architecture, the "golden means," the "modules" of the Greeks, the "triangulation" of the Gothic builders give evidence that in the past also optical keys have existed, serving as common denominators for the working teams of early builders.

Le Corbusier was more specific in his evaluation of past works of architecture and descriptions of the lessons that the architect must learn from history. In *Towards a New Architecture*, written in 1923 and considered to be one of the most influential documents in shaping the Modern movement, he wrote the following:

> The Parthenon is a product of selection applied to an established standard. Already for a century the Greek temple had been standardized in all its parts. When once a standard is established, competition comes at once and violently into play. It is a fight; in order to win you must do better than your rival in every minute point, in the run of the whole thing and in all the details. Thus we get the study of the minute points pushed to the limits. Progress.

In a section of the book entitled "The Lesson of Rome," Le Corbusier indicates specifically how the modern architect ought to learn from the past.

> Pompeii must be seen appealing in its rectangular plan. They had conquered Greece and, like good barbarians, they found the Corinthian order more beautiful than the Doric, because it was more ornate. On then with the acanthus capitals, and the entablatures decorated with little discretion or taste! But underneath this there was something Roman, as we shall see. Briefly, they constructed superb chassis, but they designed deplorable coachwork rather like the landaus of Louis XIV. Outside Rome, where there was space, they built Hadrian's Villa. One can meditate there on the greatness of Rome. There, they really planned. It is the first example of Western planning on a grand scale.

These are hardly manifestos calling for a rejection of the past. They demand, instead, a thorough understanding of the underlying factors that have generated architectural forms throughout history. This understanding permits architecture that is being shaped by dramatically changing social and technological factors to retain its position within the continuity of architectural history. This stands in marked contrast to an architecture that seeks to establish its ties to cultural continuity through the use of evocative motifs and decorations borrowed from otherwise unrelated sources.

Ms. Huxtable's article implies that one of the tenets of Modernism is that beauty in architecture results from the coldly analytical execution of mathematical and technological principals, and that all elements that cannot be justified on the basis of functional utility are to be eliminated from the work of the Moderns. In 1937 Gropius wrote:

My intention is not to introduce a, so to speak, cut and dried "Modern Style" from Europe, but to introduce a method of approach which allows one to tackle a problem according to its particular conditions.

In a 1953 talk delivered at the Illinois Institute of Technology he indicated continuing adherence to this point of view, saying:

The strong desire to include every vital component of life instead of excluding part of them for the sake of too narrow and too dogmatic an approach has characterized my whole life.

One of the most quoted and misunderstood statements relating to utilitarianism in Modern architecture comes from *Towards a New Architecture.* In the chapter "Eyes Which Do Not See" Le Corbusier states, "A house is a machine for living in." This has been taken to be a call for ultimate utilitarianism.

However, anyone who has taken the trouble to read Le Corbusier thoroughly will know that by "living" he includes much more than just satisfying basic human functions.

From the introduction:

The business of Architecture is to establish emotional relationships by means of raw materials.
Architecture goes beyond utilitarian needs.
Architecture is a plastic thing.
The spirit of order, a unity of intention.
The sense of relationships; architecture deals with quantities.
Passion can create drama out of inert stone.

And later:

You employ stone, wood and concrete, and with these materials you build houses and palaces. That is construction. Ingenuity is at work.

But suddenly you touch my heart, you do me good. I am happy and I say: "This is beautiful." That is architecture. Art enters in.

My house is practical. I thank you, as I might thank Railway engineers, or the Telephone service. You have not touched my heart.

But suppose that walls rise toward heaven in such a way I am moved. I perceive your intentions. . . . This is architecture.

Ms. Huxtable states that " . . . there were laws, written and unwritten. Ornamentation was crime." Yet there can be no question that the works of Le Corbusier make extensive use of ornamentation. This ornamentation, however, evolved from the social and technological environment of the particular building. It was not decorative motifs borrowed from some earlier and unrelated body of architecture. *Towards a New Architecture* discusses in great length the need to develop a visually satisfying building that is integrally related to an architecture evolving in a rapidly changing environment.

Architecture has nothing to do with the various "styles." The styles of Louis XIV, XV, XVI or Gothic are to architecture what a feather is on a woman's head; it is sometimes pretty, though not always, and never anything more.

Architecture is stifled by custom. The "styles" are a lie. Style is a unity of principle animating all the work of an epoch, the result of a state of mind which has its own special character: Our own epoch is determining, day by day, its own style.

The arguments of Le Corbusier have been taken as justification for "style" based entirely on the expression of technology. It is worth noting that in 1923, he cautioned against the unthinking adoption of such a simplistic approach to as complex a problem as architecture.

One commonplace among Architects (the younger ones): the construction must be shown.

Another commonplace amongst them: when a thing responds to need, it is beautiful.

But . . . to show the construction is all very well for an Arts and Crafts student who is anxious to show his ability.

The Almighty has clearly shown our ankles and our wrists, but there remains all the rest.

It is quite true that the architect should have construction at least as much at his fingers' ends as a thinker his grammar. And construction being a much more difficult and complex science than grammar, an architect's efforts are concentrated on it for a large part of his career; but he should not vegetate there.

There was certainly no intention to take aesthetic invention out of architecture, provided that invention grew from the fundamental problems with which the architect dealt. It was the use of formalized style as the primary generator of building forms against which the moderns revolted. Again, from *Towards a New Architetcure*:

We must clear up a misunderstanding.
We are in a diseased state because we mix up art with a respectful attitude towards mere decoration. This is to displace the natural feeling for art and to mingle it with a reprehensible light-mindedness in everything, which works to the advantage of the theories and campaigns conducted by "decorators" who do not understand their own period.

The modern architect, although profoundly influenced by a thorough understanding of the primary formal generators of the past, was to develop buildings that grew in all aspects, including form, space, and decoration, from the particular problem it was to solve, and from the particular social and physical environment in which it was created.

Gropius, too, was profoundly concerned with avoiding a narrow, dogmatic interpretation of the goals of modern architecture. In 1954 he wrote the following:

It is just as easy to create a modern straitjacket as a Tudor one—particularly if the architect approaches his task solely with the intention of creating a memorial to his own genius. The arrogant misapprehension of what a good architect should be often prevailed, even after the revolution against eclecticism had already set in. Designers who were searching for new expression in design would even outdo the eclecticist by striving to be "different," to seek the unique, the unheard of, the stunt.

And from Le Corbusier:

> *A seriously-minded architect, looking at it as an architect (i.e., a creator of organisms) will find in a steamship his freedom from the age-long but contemptible enslavement to the past. He will prefer respect for the forces of nature to lazy respect for tradition; to the narrowness of commonplace conceptions he will prefer the majesty of solutions of mighty efforts which has taken a giant step forward.*
>
> *When a problem is properly stated, in our epoch, it inevitably finds its solution. The problem of the house has not yet been stated.*

It is here that the essence of the Modern movement lies. There is no predetermination of form, surface, or decoration of a building based on previously established ideals of style. Rather, the building will be generated by the collective effects of the programmatic function that it is to accommodate, the technologies that are employed in its execution, the natural environmental conditions it seeks to ameliorate, and the cultural environment in which it is created. It is only an integrated solution to all of these consideration that will approach the goals set by the "Moderns of the '20s."

Ironically, regarding cultural responsiveness, the work of Robert Venturi owes its very existence to the modern pioneers. Its "style" grows directly from the Pop artists, just as Rietveld's work had a profound De Stijl sensibility and many of Le Corbusier's buildings reference forms that first appeared in Cubist and Purist painting. However, to be successful in terms of the standards established by the Moderns, the building must do much more the simply reflect the current cultural or artistic thinking. It must be shaped by all of the factors involved with its making.

It is at this juncture that we find the fundamental split in architectural points of view between the "Moderns of the '20s" and today's "young Turks."

The translation into building of the concepts developed by Gropius, Le Corbusier, and many other modern leaders has ranged from magnificently successful to disappointing. This is characteristic of the work of any movement or period. There were few Le Corbusiers in the Modern movement, and there are few Venturis among the new eclecticists. One finds, however, a seriousness of purpose, of intent, even in the less successful works of the committed Moderns that gives these buildings a social footing and an aesthetic coherence. This stands in marked contrast to the failures of the style-generated schools of architecture. When these fail as style, they fail entirely; when they succeed, the success in limited to the scope of the intentions.

Ms. Huxtable's article sees the work of Robert Venturi as a serious attack on an architectural philosophy that traces directly back to the Modern concepts of the 1920s and is, therefore, an attack

on these basic concepts. In fact, the architecture that Venturi's work confronts—the architecture that "produced so much inhumanity" and created "a million sterile downtown renewals" bears little conceptual kinship to the Modern movement, with the possible exception of some superficial appearances. The buildings that the new eclecticists attack are not buildings that respond sensitively to their environments, natural, built, or cultural. They are not shaped by the problems that they are asked to solve. They are buildings executed in a "modern style" but are not Modern buildings. The counter-revolution suggested by the article is simply an attempt to replace one twentieth-century academy with another.

It is true that architecture today is confronted with two strikingly divergent alternatives. On the one hand, there is the postwar mainstream consisting of buildings that have been determined by one of a number of styles including the Miesian glass box, concrete brutalism, neo-international style, shingle shed, and new-eclecticism. On the other hand, there are the buildings that have been shaped by the human activities they accommodate, by patterns of sun and wind movement, by changing sets of social circumstances, and by the sensitive use of technology.

For the past twenty years, mainstream architecture has relied on the underlying belief within our society that we have the resources to build whatever and as much as we want, and that technology can overcome any problems we create for ourselves through our building activities. The serious shortages that now confront us demand a thorough reevaluation of this premise. The present debate

among architectural critics regarding the merit of the new-eclecticists ignores both the role of architecture as a socially useful art and the demands architectural decisions place on the society as a whole.

The so-called radical changes espoused by the new-eclecticists are changes in style only. The "idols" that they topple are straw men which they have themselves erected. They do not confront the issues of modernism of the 1920s but simply attack a "modern style" of the '50s with the notion of replacing it with an "eclectic style" of the '70s.

Our daily experience tells us that most of the body of architecture produced since the early 1950s has done little to enhance our quality of life. Rather, it has put tremendous demands on what have turned out to be limited resources—economic, natural, environmental, and human—while offering little in return. This architecture is not the conceptual descendant of the modernism of the 1920s but instead a reestablishment of an architecture in which intellectual games of style are played for the amusement of the cognoscenti. The choice architecture now faces is not one of eclecticism versus Purism, one style versus another. It is rather a question of what is to determine basic architectural decisions—style, or the specifics of the time, place, and function from which the building evolves. There seems little point in discussing one style or another at a time when fundamental directions must be established. The turning point at which architecture finds itself today is centered on whether to continue the architecture of styles that has predominated for the past twenty years or to reestablish a true Modernism.

The history of Modernism contains numerous examples of sustainable strategies, particularly with regard to the controlled use of the sun. Also, and perhaps more important, it suggests a mindset and discipline which in the context of current global issues will support holistic, environmental action.

3.3

Modernism and Sustainability

Why is Modernist thought intrinsic to the development of green strategies for both existing as well as new buildings? The Modern movement in architecture evolved concurrently with attitudes in the arts and sciences in which the clear statement and exploration of issues and problems was integral to the creative process and in which the end products were profoundly shaped by the process itself. While this is not unique to the Moderns, their insistence on the hierarchical difference between the products of serious analysis and those of casual appliqué has profound importance to our current situation.

A sustainable future, one in which humankind will have a place in the ecosystem of the earth, depends on a fundamental reconsideration of how we utilize all of the resources that support the qualities of our lives. The earth is essentially a finite system. The limits of nonrenewable resources are obvious. Renewable resources are limited by the rate at which they are received and by the environmental disruption caused by their capture and use. There are limited amounts of waste that the earth can accommodate before environmental conditions change to the point that current life patterns become untenable. Each new demand on limited resources creates additional pressures on other critical areas. There is a finite amount of arable land on the planet. We have already seen that initial, small steps from petroleum to biofuels produced dramatic effects on the cost and availability of food. There is no quick fix. There is no technological fix. What is required is a change in our fundamental approach to providing quality of life—from basic survival to the highest planes of culture and spirit.

While advances in science and technology will certainly address many of the problems we are now confronting as we move ever nearer to the limiting conditions of resource availability, they will take decades to implement and will have issues we do not yet fully understand. The one broad strategy that can produce immediate, meaningful results is to do more with less. This, in turn, requires we first be clear about what we need to "do more" of. A Modernist perspective offers some guidelines.

In *Towards a New Architecture*, Le Corbusier wrote:

The lesson of the airplane lies in the logic which governed the statement of the problem and its realization. The problem of the house has not yet been stated.

This could be brought up to date and expanded: The problem of architecture has not yet been stated. In the early twentieth century, paramount issues driving Modern architectural theory included the effects of science and technology applied directly to rapidly changing social and cultural canvases. The industrial revolution had matured to the point that its effects were widely integrated into Western production, offering a vastly increased architectural palette. Advances in mechanical and electrical systems created an entirely new set of vertical options. They also effectively decoupled the interior requirements for light and ventilation from the outside environment. Science provided a new view of the universe, incorporating the interrelationship of space and time. Cubism used this conceptualization as the underlying idea of a major body of paintings and collages, thereby transforming science into cultural expression. The topology of architecture and planning was radically altered by the conceptualization of time as a dimension, enabling the superposition of objects in plan, elevation, and section.

But unlike painting, this new topology applied to the realities inherent to architecture produced not only new forms and spaces but also new opportunities for addressing how people work and live. (See 8.3, "Cubism, Sculpture, and Architecture.")

Twentieth-century Modernism developed as a direct response to new and profound understandings that had emerged in the early 1900s. A current application of the Modern process must incorporate the impact of two relatively recent phenomena—the realization of the finiteness of physical resources, and the remarkable advances in information management. Fortunately, the Modern process is highly accepting of changing criteria; however, to move forward effectively, it is important to understand the historical and cultural contexts of early Modernism. Although the iconic scientific and cultural pillars of Modernism—the theories of Relativity and Cubism—appear in the early twentieth century, much of the preliminary spadework can be seen beginning in the mid-nineteenth century. Modernism could not have evolved without these key physical, technological, cultural, and scientific precedents. (See 8.8, "Cities, Energy, and Architecture.") Similarly, the current recognition and analysis of the fundamental drivers of the crisis in environmental and sustainability issues were explicitly noted by the mid-1960s. *The Limits to Growth*, the 1972 report of the Club of Rome project,

documents a comprehensive study undertaken in 1968. Two profound points in this remarkable analysis are its identification of the time frame of the finite resource crisis, and a formulation, albeit tacit, of "sustainability." The first summary point in the introduction reads:

> *If the present growth trends in world population, industrialization, pollution, food production, and resource depletion continue unchanged, the limits to growth on this planet will be reached sometime within the next one hundred years.*

This was written forty years ago. The Club of Rome analyses that follow suggested that the leading edge of this ecological upheaval would become apparent in the first few years of the twenty-first century, a remarkably prescient projection. Also in the introduction is a discussion of the relationship between the problems inherent in these limits and the extents, both in space and time, of the context in which they are viewed. Space begins with "family" (although it might have started with self), expands to "business, city, neighborhood," "race, nation," and finally "world." Time begins with "next week" (although it might have started with the next second or minute), runs to "next few years," "lifetime," and "children's lifetime." It goes on to say that the human concerns that guide our actions tend to be those associated with the smallest space and shortest time frames, but that these have effects that are far more vast. There is an immense gulf between the scale of the criteria on which our actions are based and the impacts that result from those actions.

When we choose to operate an electrical device, we may consider the utility bill that will have to be paid later in the month. We may, in times of stressed utility capacity, realize that this operation may contribute to a system overload resulting in brownouts or blackouts. It is unusual, however, to visualize the contribution that the decision to operate an electrical device makes to the plume of smoke and carbon dioxide leaving the stack of a generator three hundred miles away or to the added demand for coal with its related environmental degradation. We don't think about the part, however small, that our use of electricity plays in the deaths of thirty to forty coal miners each year in the United States.

It is also unusual to consider the future environmental or ecological effects of current actions. How will the lives of my grandchildren be affected by the electric consumption of the computer that I'm using at this moment? The Iroquois Confederacy had a basic tenet that its leaders consider the

impact of every important decision on the seventh generation yet to come. When context and technology are relatively stable, a seven-generation view is feasible. In our current, rapidly changing world, it seems impossible to anticipate the effects that our decisions will have on our great-great-great-great-great-grandchildren. However, even an anticipation of the world of our great-grandchildren, say the last quarter of the twenty-first century, will be a strong beginning for a sustainable ethos.

Of course, an ethos will not in and of itself change our impact on the planet. What it will do is provide a set of reference points for the evaluation of alternatives, alternatives which must be developed, quantified,and qualified through rigorous scientific, technological, and cultural understanding. This is the Modern process.

This raises a question: Does making choices and getting along with less imply a reduction in quality of life? There has been an effort to characterize Modernism as sterile and inhuman. Much of this is the result of an honest misunderstanding of the Modern movement; however, much is the result of a very conscious effort to trivialize the importance of an analytic, rational process as the base for planning our built environment. Perhaps the barb most often thrown at Modern architecture is the quote from Le Corbusier, taken out of context: "The house is a machine for living in." On the surface, this would appear to suggest a mechanistic view of the relationship between house and occupant. This famous line, first published in *Towards a New Architecture*, is part of a chapter dealing with lessons to be learned from aircraft design. Yet as noted earlier, the same book opens each of three

above, opposite, and overleaf
The ocher pigments in the rocks and earth in and around Roussillon, France, provide a distinctive counterpoint to the otherwise verdant landscape, inform local design sensibilities, and also become the actual coloring agents of the built environment affecting everything from the broad townscape to the smallest details. Logical efficiencies, economic and environmental, create the defining element of this regional architecture.

chapters under the heading "Architecture" with a passionate plea for and defense of the sublime as a guiding concept of architecture. The passage " . . . you have established certain relationships which have aroused my emotions. This is architecture" has profound importance in understanding both the fundamental intentions of Modernism and their distortion in modern style works.

This view of architecture, from the same publication as "the house is a machine for living in," is far from dry and utilitarian. To the contrary, it is a call for architects to address emotions, passion, and spirit, to create Art. As soon as "living" includes activities of the mind, the two definitions become completely consistent, inextricably connected.

The "machine" is to satisfy the needs and wants of emotion and spirit as well as those of intellect and body. The failure, whether intentional or accidental, to interpret the "machine for living" phrase in the context of this passage is at the heart of the fundamental misrepresentation of Modernism, a misrepresentation that directly led to an unfortunate return to the consideration of architecture as form-making, and thus inherently ecologically damaging.

Why has this seemingly obvious misrepresentation been overlooked for so long? One reason is that its application would argue against much of the basis for contemporary marketing and commerce; the concept of "more stuff" is sold as being better

than "less stuff." Yet beyond basic needs, emotion and spirit are addressed more by quality than by quantity. And while "stuff" per se does little to meet the criteria that Le Corbusier put forth as the bases for architecture, the concept of "stuff" can easily be sold.

On the surface, this seems to raise a contradiction between the goals of Modern architecture and sustainability. If architecture is a valid endeavor, and if our architecture is to create "machines for living in" or "machines for working in" or "machines for learning in" or "machines for healing in" or "machines for becoming enlightened in," and if we recognize that each of these activities is an important component of human existence, does this not create a demand for construction, and isn't construction inherently environmentally destructive? It is here that the subtleties inherent in the Modern process are most valuable. If we recognize that resources are finite but that meeting a wide range of human needs is essential, a fundamental criterion in selecting alternatives for making places for living, working, learning, healing, and enlightening is the understanding of how to achieve these ends in ways that address the similar needs of future generations. Just as Modernism of the early twentieth century drew on the products and processes of industrialization, the vision of Cubism, the spatial conceptualization of relativity, so Modernism of the early twenty-first century must draw on concern for sustainability and on the understanding of the full range of options for its achievement.

Will we have to give things up, make sacrifices? To some degree, yes; however, a characteristic of all life, including the human species, is a ready willingness—whether by hard-wired response or conscious decision—to nurture, to do what is necessary to insure not only continued survival of our species, our culture, and our families, but also to see that they thrive. As a species, as cultures, as professionals, and as individuals, cultivating the future is a primary imperative.

But this still asks: Does this mean a lesser quality of life today? And again, a Modernist construct is invaluable in showing that thinking sustainably will, in many ways, improve our current condition as well as that of the future. It begins with a fundamental restatement of the "why" of architecture. The purpose of architecture is not, at its heart, to make buildings. Rather, it is to provide the places—the machines—that at least allow, and preferably enhance and encourage, the full range of activities of our lives. We need to reconsider these essential activities of our lives in the context of the rapid loss of the physical elements, both built and natural, that created and were created by our cultural history. Not surprisingly, this condition has led to an increasing awareness of the differences between true experience and simulation. The term *authenticity* is ever more widely used in the search for improved or meaningful endeavor.

In architecture, we need to decide whether the end purpose is the building itself or the building as a

means to engage broader aspects of our lives. From a slightly different perspective, each architectural undertaking relates to its context somewhat differently, but in general, the building may be considered an independent object, an object placed into a context as a picture into a frame, or a new component that alters but becomes integral to the context. Context may be physical or cultural. It may be a landscape or cityscape or it may be the activities of our lives. The ultimate effect of planning and architectural activity results from the interactions between object and context. Understanding this is at the heart of Modern sustainable practice. Often, less building, less incursion into the context, will produce a better result, not only in reducing environmental damage but also in creating enhanced qualitative experiences. A spare, efficient solution can provide experiences that would be masked and overwhelmed by a less elegant response. Understanding the interrelationship between context—

opposite and below
The natural pattern of the rocks in the cliffs of Chaco Canyon, New Mexico is mirrored in the constructed stonework of the pre-Columbian Chetro Ketl pueblo, ca. 945–1090.

natural and cultural—is integral to maintaining
and reinforcing genius loci, sense of place. In other
words, "less may be more" is not just a concept or
abstraction, but a means to more fully enjoy our
rich and complex world.

Modernism provides the philosophical and analytic
bases for architecture and planning in which design
decisions are based on specific criteria. Recognition of the finiteness of resources, the global
homogenization place and culture, and the rise of
virtual experience reinforce the primacy of authentic experience as one of these criteria. The adoption
of this criterion leads to architecture and planning
in which a more satisfying quality of life is achieved
with less demand on the environment.

above left
Preservation of the historic street wall reinforces
cultural continuity and reuses valuable resources
in place. London, 1991.

above right and opposite
On East 67th Street in New York City, streetscape
continuity, physical and chronological, was main-
tained by incorporating complete Victorian
street walls into new state-of-the-art combined
police and fire facilities. TSP/Elemental Architecture, 1990.

The tenets of Modernism, applied to early twenty-first century conditions, will demand that preservation and adaptive reuse be a primary component in any comprehensive program to meet the needs of our built environment. Conceptual Modernism also offers a very specific framework for evaluating and executing preservation projects.

3.4

Modernism and Preservation

Modernism, often seen to be at odds with building preservation, is integral to the effective reuse of the vast inventory of existing buildings as well as to the preservation of many historic and landmark-quality structures. The relationship between Modernism and preservation is twofold. A Modernist platform will inform the degree to which repair and restoration techniques should be historically based, but where nonhistoric restoration is appropriate, a Modern discipline will provide the analytic tools to support reconstruction that employs technological advances, from design tools to materials and fabrication.

However the connections between Modernism and building preservation extend far deeper. From a planning perspective, a Modern analysis of our current situation begins with recognition that limited resource availability is a primary constraint to any systemic solution to problems facing the physical environment, built and natural. Thus, key to any strategy will be optimization of resource use. This includes the evaluation of not only the quantity of resources—how much material will be

employed—but also of the quality. This is a question of economic cost as well as one of environmental measurement. One readily available metric is energy. There is substantial, quantified information regarding U.S. energy use. Actual energy use for building operation is constantly being recorded by electric and gas meters and made manifest in fuel bills. (See 4.1, "Energy: A Measure of Sustainability.")

However, it is also important to recognize that the conditions suggested by energy figures are representative of, if not directly transferable to, all aspects of our existence. Obtaining raw materials will have an inevitable impact on the natural environment. Increasing scarcity will force the exploitation of ever more sensitive and difficult-to-obtain resources. Just as it takes additional energy to raise the quality of a set quantity of energy, raising the quality of any resource requires the commitment of secondary resources that do not, in themselves, become part of the primary resource. For example, the environmental value or cost of the cement, sand, gravel, water, iron ore, and alloying metals in their natural state is far less than the same materi-

als in a fully constructed reinforced concrete building frame. (See 4.5, "Energy Quality: The Second Law of Thermodynamics.")

There are strong quantitative bases for insisting on reuse and preservation as a primary strategy for meeting the needs of the built environment. There are also significant qualitative benefits to building preservation, particularly in reinforcing sense of place and connection to cultural and historic continuity. These criteria must be considered in conjunction with the quantitative, an optimized solution being one that integrates all of the considerations into a seamless whole.

Modernism gives an outline, if not the final, fully developed tools, for the evaluation of the reuse of existing structures within a comprehensive context. The concept of a matrix that displays the interrelationships between many diverse demands, solutions, and techniques remains a valuable tool. There is, however, a danger in viewing such a tool as constrictive or dehumanizing, as is the case of a simple programming matrix in which each space is defined as either related or nonrelated to every other space—a black or white condition. The benefits or drawbacks of building reuse, for example, are generally not so sharply drawn. A degree of subtlety can be introduced to the same matrix by the use of numerical values to represent the importance of the interrelationship at each cell. While this adds a level of refinement, the information within each cell and the characteristics of the interrelationships

above
Castello Sforzesco,
Milan, ca. 1395.
Renovation BBPR, ca. 1950.

opposite
Combined Police/Five Facilities,
New York City. TSP/Elemental, 1991.

are still limited to a graduated variation of the yes or no condition. The Moderns recognized that it was necessary to do more than simply state that a relationship existed. The CIAM grid uses a number of devices, including words and numbers, drawings and photographs, to give depth and qualitative information regarding the relationships identified by the matrix process. (See 8.5, "CIAM Grid.")

Of course, the CIAM grid was developed well before the advent of digital information. Computers offer the possibility of managing information at levels inconceivable to the members of the Congrès Internationaux d'Architecture Moderne. While this facilitates the incorporation not only of data but also of many other forms of information, it also becomes a filter. Digital information tends to separate individual items from the overall view, in contrast to a physical grid, which remains in full view even as one is examining a particular cell. Modernism demands that we establish methodologies that allow one to

zoom in and out without losing comprehension of the full context.

While Modernism does not, in itself, offer new design tools for building reuse and historic preservation, it does provide a very clear framework for the appropriate application of these tools. The reconstruction of Shepard Hall at the City College of New York, carried out as a series of publicly bid, lump-sum contracts, was only possible through the extensive use of computer modeling and data management. The project involves the insertion of totally new structure in significant parts of the building as well as the fabrication and installation of over 70,000 replicas to replace severely deteriorated terra cotta. The ornamental surfaces of the building are treated as a complex rainscreen, and distinct addresses are established for each of the replacement units. Digital models of each piece are created and virtually assembled prior to the start of the physical manufacturing process. (See 9.2, "Shepard Hall.")

Building preservation employs resources at their highest level by adapting and reusing existing structures in place rather than demolishing and replacing them. Environmental benefits result from eliminating the need to commit or upgrade new resources.

3.5

Preservation and Sustainability

The postwar history of building preservation and sustainable design are closely intertwined. Design concerns for the elegant, efficient use of materials, intrinsic to Modernism, led to the quantification of embodied energy, the energy in building construction. Realization of the significance of the embodied energy in historic buildings has become one of the arguments for their preservation. Increased awareness of the need for wise utilization of all resources has resulted in the incorporation of building upgrades and adaptive reuse into many sustainable building standards. For example, the Leadership in Energy and Environmental Design (LEED) program of the U.S. Green Building Council awards three credits for the reuse in place of existing building material. This represents about ten percent of the total number of credits required for certification. LEED-defined community benefits, such as meeting minimum density requirements and offering proximity to public services and transportation, add an additional three credits, and are frequently realized when existing buildings are reused.

It is no accident that James Marston Fitch, widely considered the founder of modern architectural preservation, subtitled the reissue of his encyclopedic history of U.S. architecture *American Building: The Environmental Forces That Shape It*. It is also no accident that Jim Fitch, educated at Tulane in the 1920s and having begun his career restoring antebellum mansions, considered himself a Modernist or that he saw contemporary preservation as a very Modern calling.

There are many measurable benefits to preservation, including reduced energy use, carbon release, and landfill material. There is also quantifiable job creation, which is greater per dollar spent for renovation than for new construction. There are also qualitative benefits, including community preservation and reinforcement of sense of place. Buildings and sites that are important cultural and historical artifacts must be preserved for their iconic and symbolic significance regardless of other considerations. The authentic historic value cannot be re-created in new construction, regardless of economic or environmental expenditure.

The relative weight placed on quantitative and qualitative considerations in deciding whether to

reuse a building or demolish and replace it is not absolute but rather exists on a sliding scale. At one end are the truly important artifacts. These will be protected and preserved no matter what the cost. The decision-making process will be almost entirely based on qualitative factors. At the other end of the scale are buildings that are seen to have little or no value beyond their ability to enclose space and accommodate programmatic usage. Whether or not these will be saved will be determined almost entirely by quantitative analysis. Will reusing the building save money, reduce energy use, carbon release, and so forth? The problem arises with the vast number of existing buildings that fall in the midrange of the scale. These are the relatively anonymous buildings that form the bulk of our towns and cities, or that have some historical importance but were not home to watershed events. There is no way to directly evaluate contribution to sense of place against gallons of oil required for preservation, yet this is the challenge faced in most cases where building reuse is one of several options being considered. Here, decisions will not be determined by comparing numbers or comparing scores. Some form of consensus will be required, however, for this to be meaningful, all of the factors must be clearly presented to all stakeholders. Although there are precedents that suggest a general direction, such as the CIAM grid, new tools are required to address contemporary issues and with these tools, judgment is needed. (See 8.5, "CIAM Grid.")

Above all, a contemporary Modernist approach, which recognizes the critical issues of the twenty-first century as well as the qualitative values embedded in the vast stock of mid-scale buildings, will insist that reuse and upgrade be a primary strategy to the provision of built space. This is in contrast to the attitudes of the last several generations, which has generally considered new construction as the primary task of architecture, with preservation and reuse as minor sidelines. The default approach to meeting human needs has been to create new space from the ground up, often demolishing buildings to obtain clear land. This must be changed. The starting point must be to determine whether there is existing building stock that can be modified to meet new program and performance yardsticks and to create new buildings only when needs cannot be met through reuse and preservation. This approach will not only capitalize on the qualitative assets of existing buildings but will also enhance the appreciation of and value placed on new construction.

A new paradigm is needed.

Topping out the recon-
struction of the Main Tower.
Shepard Hall, City College
of New York. TSP/Elemental
Architectural, 1991.

4

Energy
and
Sustainability

Understanding energy is integral to designing a sustainable world. While energy usage is only one aspect, albeit a critical one, of environmentally conscious design, it can also serve as a proxy for virtually any finite resource.

Directly or indirectly, energy usage imposes the single greatest demand on and damage to our ecosystem. Energy usage is a significant factor in the application of virtually all other resources. The behavior and effects of energy, as described by the Laws of Thermodynamics, mirror closely the behavior of all resources.

4.1

Energy: A Measure of Sustainability

Throughout this book, discussions of energy stand for discussions of the larger physical environment, particularly as it is affected by the commitment of resources. Despite the fact that energy use is only one factor that impacts the environment, it remains a very useful model for understanding many other issues.

Energy is broadly relevant in that there is almost no physical resource use that does not result in the commitment of energy. There is an extensive body of data on energy transactions throughout our economy, from raw resources to delivered finished product. The patterns of energy use are well understood. Energy provides a good basis for tracking the flow of materials, products, and services throughout the economy much as a marker dye displays movement within a fluid.

The broad impacts of using any resource closely follow those of energy use, whether or not they are specifically quantifiable. All resources, whether renewable or nonrenewable, are finite. For all practical purposes, nonrenewable resources are finite in absolute quantity. Whatever currently exists is all that there is. No more will be added within a meaningful time frame. They may be moved, processed, changed in form, and rearranged, but they will not be replaced. Renewable resources are limited by the rate at which they can be renewed.

Preparation of formwork and reinforcing for one of the 32 precast concrete "drums" which form the cores of the four reconstructed turrets at Shepard Hall, City College of New York. TSP/Elemental Architecture, 1986–present.

The continued growth of global demand is rapidly approaching, in some cases has exceeded, the capacity of the planet to produce, or reproduce, these resources. These are essentially First Law or quantitative considerations. (See 4.5, "Energy Quantity: The First Law of Thermodynamics.")

The quality of a resource will affect its utility and its value, but raising the quality of a resource will impose its own set of environmental demands. A brick that is part of a brick wall possesses exactly the same amount of material as an equivalently sized lump of clay in the ground, but its value is substantially greater. This value may be defined in many ways, including economic measurement, increase in utility, or resource or environmental cost. These are often, but not necessarily, closely linked. For the clay to become brick and part of the wall, it must be taken from the ground, transported to a brick plant, shaped, fired in a kiln, transported to the job site, lifted to its place on the wall, and assembled. In terms of actual material, there is very little difference between the clay in the ground and the brick incorporated into the wall, yet the difference in its usefulness to humankind is profound. The two conditions also impose very different environmental demands. This phenomenon is not unlike the external energy that must be used to raise a lower form of energy, such as heat, to a higher form, such as electricity. The transformation is qualitative and is a Second Law phenomenon. (See 4.6, "Energy Quality: The Second Law of Thermodynamics.")

above
Each concrete "drum" is transported from Western Pennsylvania, approximately 250 miles.

opposite
Each "drum" must be hoisted to its eventual location on the building, between 100 and 150 feet above street level.

above and opposite

Structural cores of the turrets in place before installation of
cladding. At each of the four turrets, the first drum is anchored
to a new "foundation" 100 feet above street level, followed
by seven more drums. These are all laced together to form
"masts" 6 feet in diameter by 50 feet in height.

While energy comprises much of the added resources needed to raise the value—economic, environmental, utilitarian—of a lump of clay in the ground to that of a brick in a building wall, other resources, including human labor, must also be added. Each of these also has economic and environmental dimensions. For example, people making bricks occupy space on the planet, need food and shelter, consume water, and produce waste. (See 5.6 Waste Management.")

An increase in the use of human labor will eventually require an increase in population. That increase in population will place demands on the environment as well as on renewable and nonrenewable resources. On the other hand, when unemployment is a concern, an understanding of the impact of alternative decisions on the need for jobs is a valuable planning tool.

When the brick wall is demolished and the brick ends up in a landfill or the ocean, the clay still exists, but there has been a substantial reduction in its value, again whether measured in economic or environmental terms. If, after demolition, a similar brick wall was built using salvaged materials from the original, new energy would have to be introduced to clean and reassemble the bricks and for new mortar; however, the energy and resources that had been used for the manufacture and transportation of the bricks themselves would be recaptured.

This example is representative of virtually every aspect of the physical environment. The current stock of buildings embodies immense quantities of high-quality resources. If we are serious about pursuing sustainable strategies for our built environment, there is no question that the informed reuse of existing structures will be a primary component of any plan.

above and opposite
Structural cores of the turrets in place before installation of cladding. The economic and environmental value of the concrete elements making up these structural cores is many times that of the concrete itself.

above
Turrets with new cladding.

opposite
Blocks of concrete which have a volume
of material roughly equivalent to one
"drum" installed on the building, yet have
significantly lower Second Law value.

Embodied energy is the total energy resource committed to produce a specific result, whether a service or a product. It includes the energy for extracting and processing raw materials, manufacturing components, and installation. It includes the transportation energy used throughout the entire production cycle and the energy consumed by the service activities that support the process. It includes the energy resources that become physically part of the finished product, such as the petroleum in asphalt paving, and the energy used in the offices where the planning, design, and project management are carried out.

4.2

Embodied Energy

One of the strongest reasons for upgrading and continuing to use the vast inventory of existing buildings is to exploit the value that results from the commitment of the resources used to make these structures, the embodied resources. Because of the direct and indirect environmental impacts and because of the widely available data, embodied energy is currently the primary quantifiable criterion for embodied resource evaluation and will continue to be so for at least the next several decades. (See 4.1, "Energy: A Measure of Sustainability.")

The sheer magnitude of embodied energy in new building construction becomes, in itself, a compelling argument for the continued use or adaptive reuse of existing building stock. Although it requires energy to renovate and upgrade, the reuse in place of much of the basic materials—steel, concrete, masonry, and perhaps glass, wood, finishes, and so forth—continues the productive application of these resources at their elevated value and offsets the need to commit new resources for their replacement. The energy used by new building construc-

tion in the United States represents approximately 5 percent of all domestic energy consumption. This could be cut in half through a program of building reuse in lieu of demolition and replacement. Such a program, including comprehensive performance upgrade, would yield a significant increase in construction jobs per dollar spent.

The most recent comprehensive analysis of embodied energy and the associated impact on job creation in the U.S. construction industry was compiled in 1981. Although some processes have changed, such as a dramatic increase in the use of recycled aluminum, we can still use that data to inform some overall attitudes toward meeting our building needs. (See 4.3, "A Handbook of Embodied Energy in Building Construction.")

More recently, a 2007 study comparing renovation of Marcel Breuer's Cleveland Trust Tower with demolishing and replacing it indicated that building reuse would save about half of the total embodied energy. These savings considered the embodied energy costs for the comprehensive upgrades

required to have the building operate at the same performance levels as a contemporary, high-performance structure. (See 9.1, "Embodied Energy in the Cleveland Trust Tower.")

Applied to office buildings in general, these savings would be the equivalent of approximately five to seven gallons of oil per square foot, roughly the amount of energy it would take to operate the building for five to ten years. From a different perspective, if one were to consider a twenty-year life-cycle analysis, this saving in energy for construction would be equivalent to a saving 25–50 percent of the operating energy.

Rank Order	399 Order	Name	Trillion Btu	Fraction	Cumulative Fraction
1	3	Refined petroleum	57.34	21.83	21.83
2	240	Fab structural steel	24.97	9.50	31.33
3	206	Ready-mix concrete	19.51	7.43	38.76
4	241	Metal doors	10.47	3.98	42.74
5	245	Misc metal work	7.37	2.81	44.55
6	243	Sheet metal work	7.13	2.72	48.27
7	217	Steel products	6.97	2.65	50.92
8	196	Bricks	6.50	2.47	53.39
9	230	Nonferrous wire	6.49	2.47	55.86
10	372	Wholesale trade	5.61	2.13	57.99
11	204	Concrete blocks	4.86	1.85	59.84
12	312	Light fixtures	4.81	1.83	61.67
13	373	Retail trade	4.56	1.73	63.40
14	255	Pipe	4.22	1.61	65.05
15	205	Concrete products	4.13	1.57	66.58
16	386	Misc prof services	4.09	1.56	68.14
17	244	Arch metal work	3.85	1.47	69.61
18	193	Glass products	3.81	1.45	71.06
19	293	Refrigeration mach	3.66	1.39	72.45
20	183	Paving	3.30	1.25	73.70
21	214	Mineral wool	3.09	1.18	74.88
22	184	Asphalt	2.92	1.11	75.99
23	195	Cement	2.88	1.10	77.09
24	398	Business travel	2.85	1.09	78.18
25	182	Paint products	2.58	.98	79.16
26	242	Fab plate work	2.57	.98	80.14
27	265	Elevators	2.48	.92	81.06
28	374	Motor freight trans	2.15	.82	81.88
29	239	Heating equipment	2.14	.81	82.69
30	362	Railroad	2.09	.79	83.48
31	298	Switchgear	2.08	.79	84.27
32	188	Misc plastics	2.07	.79	85.06
33	211	Asbestos product	2.05	.78	85.84
34	250	Hardware	1.88	.71	86.55
35	4	Electric utilities	1.66	.63	87.18
36	139	Veneer, plywood	1.61	.61	87.79
37	138	Millwork	1.54	.58	88.37
38	252	Fab wire products	1.40	.57	88.94
39	152	Metal fixtures	1.41	.54	89.40
40	384	Misc business service	1.30	.50	89.98
41	227	Copper rolling	1.28	.49	90.47
42	160	Building paper	1.23	.47	90.94
43	267	Hoists, cranes	1.21	.46	91.40
44	5	Gas utilities	1.16	.44	91.84
45	208	Gypsum products	1.14	.43	92.27
46	387	Automobile repair	1.14	.43	92.70
47	174	Misc chemical prod	1.08	.41	93.11
48	215	Nonclay refractories	.90	.34	93.45
49	380	Real estate	.90	.34	93.79
50	342	Temp controls	.81	.31	94.10
51	21	Stone clay mining	.81	.31	94.41
52	197	Ceramic tile	.66	.25	94.66
53	218	Iron, steel foundries	.61	.23	94.89
54	142	Wood products	.59	.23	95.12
55	238	Plumbing fittings	.59	.22	95.34
56	313	Wiring devices	.56	.21	95.55
57	135	Sawmills	.50	.19	95.74
58	377	Insurance carriers	.50	.19	95.93
59	141	Wood preserving	.48	.18	96.11
60	307	Electric h'wares	.48	.18	96.29
61	207	Lime	.46	.17	96.46
62	237	Metal sanitary ware	.45	.17	96.63
63	199	Clay products	.44	.17	96.80
64	177	Floor coverings	.44	.17	96.97
65	151	Wood fixtures	.44	.17	97.14
66	209	Stone products	.42	.16	97.30
67	385	Advertising	.36	.14	97.44
68	228	Aluminum rolling	.34	.13	97.57
69	369	Communications	.34	.13	97.70
70	161	Conv paper products	.33	.13	97.83
71	365	Water transport	.33	.13	97.96
72	394	Nonprofit org	.33	.13	98.09
73	358	Hard floor covering	.32	.12	98.12
74	200	Plumbing fixtures	.31	.12	98.33
75	185	Tires	.29	.11	98.11
76	281	Blowers	.29	.11	98.55
		Other inputs under .1 percent each	3.71	1.45	100.00
		Total	262.70	100.00	

399 Order	Name	Fraction
3	Refined petroleum	21.83
4	Electric utilities	.63
5	Gas utilities	.44
135	Sawmills	.19
138	Millwork	.58
139	Veneer, plywood	.61
141	Wood preserving	.18
142	Wood products	.23
	Other inputs under .1 percent each	.05
182	Paint products	.98
183	Paving	1.26
184	Asphalt	1.11
195	Cement	1.09
196	Bricks	2.47
197	Ceramic tile	.25
199	Clay products	.17
200	Plumbing fixtures	.12
204	Concrete blocks	1.85
205	Concrete products	1.57
206	Ready-mix concrete	7.43
207	Lime	.17
208	Gypsum products	.43
209	Stone products	.16
211	Asbestos products	.78
214	Mineral wool	1.18
215	Nonclay refractories	.34
	Other inputs under .1 percent each	.26
217	Steel products	2.65
218	Iron, steel foundries	.23
227	Copper rolling	.49
228	Aluminum rolling	.13
230	Nonferrous wire	2.47
237	Metal sanitary ware	.17
238	Plumbing fittings	.22
239	Heating equipment	.81
240	Fab structural steel	9.50
241	Metal doors	3.98
242	Fab plate work	.98
243	Sheet metal work	2.72
244	Arch metal work	1.47
245	Misc metal work	2.81
250	Hardware	.71
252	Fab wire products	.57
255	Pipe	1.61
	Other inputs under .1 percent each	.10
362	Railroad	.79
364	Motor freight trans	.82
365	Water transport	.13
	Other inputs under .1 percent each	.11
372	Wholesale trade	2.14
373	Retail trade	1.73
384	Misc business serv	.50
385	Advertising	.14
386	Misc prof services	1.56
21	Stone, clay mining	.31
117	Floor covering	.17
151	Wood fixtures	.17
152	Metal fixtures	.54
160	Building paper	.47
161	Conv paper products	.13
174	Misc chemical prod	.41
185	Tires	.11
188	Misc plastics	.79
193	Glass products	1.45
265	Elevators	.92
267	Hoists, cranes	.46
281	Blowers	.79
293	Refrigeration mach	1.39
298	Switchgear	.79
307	Electric h'wares	.18
312	Light fixtures	1.83
313	Wiring devices	.21
342	Temp controls	.31
358	Hard floor covering	.12
369	Communications	.13
377	Insurance carriers	.19
380	Real estate	.34
387	Automobile repair	.43
394	Nonprofit org	.13
398	Business travel	1.09
	Other inputs under .1 percent each	.94

DIRECT ENERGY

WOOD

PAINT PAVING

STONE CLAY PROD

METAL PROD

TRADE

TRANSPORT

SERVICE

MISC

The Handbook of Energy Use for Building Construction, available through the U.S. National Technical Information Service, provides extensive data on the embodied energy in the building construction industry and in many specific construction products.

4.3

A Handbook of Embodied Energy in Building Construction

Published in 1981, the *Handbook* was prepared under a contract with the U.S. Department of Energy and was based on ten years of research conducted by Richard G. Stein and Dr. Bruce Hannon. It is a comprehensive presentation of patterns of energy embodiment throughout the construction industries. While changes in manufacturing processes and resource recovery have altered some of the specific data, the document remains the most complete source for this information. It identifies the total energy resources used in building construction and prorates the energy share used by each industry and service that supports the construction industry—its total embodied energy. It breaks down construction into forty-nine categories and lists the sources of energy input for each—the energy to extract, process, and transport raw materials, to manufacture and assemble, and to deliver products to the building site. It also includes the energy consumed at the building site, the direct energy. The embodied energy of the building materials plus the direct energy of construction is the embodied energy of a building in place.

Of the forty-nine categories, seventeen are new building; five are building maintenance, repair, and alteration; and the remaining twenty-seven categories are non-building (infrastructure) construction and repair. For each new building category, energy requirements are listed both on a national basis and per square foot of construction. The figures identify the energy used by all processes prior to material and product arriving at the building site, the energy embodied in those materials and products, and the energy consumed in the construction process itself. From these figures, one can estimate the energy that will typically be required to construct a particular type of building. For example, the construction of a new 100,000-square-foot school building will require 140 billion Btu, the equivalent of about one million gallons of oil. Embodied energy per square foot varies considerably among building types, from about 150,000 Btu per square foot (the equivalent of about 1 gallon of oil) for farm utility buildings to about 1,700,000 Btu (the equivalent of 11–12 gallons of oil) for hospitals.

4.2.1   Building or Common Brick (continued)

	Unit	Btu/Unit at Jobsite
Cavity wall with 4″ thick common brick (6.75 brk/sq ft) and 6″ thick concrete block backup, 6″ x 8″ x 16″ units, (1.13 blocks/sq ft) including mortar	sq ft	170,000
Cavity wall with 4″ thick common brick (6.75 brk/sq ft) and 8″ thick concrete block backup, 8″ x 8″ x 16″ units (1.13 blocks/sq ft) including mortar	sq ft	176,000
Jumbo Brick (7 5/8″ x 3 5/8″ x 7 5/8″)	1 brk	48,400
4″ Thick jumbo brick wall including mortar, (2.25 brk/sq ft)	sq ft	126,000
8″ Thick solid jumbo brick wall including mortar, (4.50 brk/sq ft)	sq ft	271,000
Cavity wall with 4″ thick jumbo brick (2.25 brk/sq ft) and 4″ thick concrete block backup, 4″ x 8″ x 16″ units, (1.13 blocks/sq ft) including mortar	sq ft	155,000
Cavity wall with 4″ thick jumbo brick (2.25 brk/sq ft) and 6″ thick concrete block backup, 6″ x 8″ x 16″ units, (1.13 blocks/sq ft) including mortar	sq ft	165,000

Sample listing of embodied energy in specific building materials from *The Handbook of Energy Use for Building Construction* (1981).

Data for each category are detailed in several different ways, including the inputs from all industries that contribute more than 0.1 percent of the total of that category. In addition, the *Handbook* lists the embodied energy in more than a thousand specific building materials and products. These are organized as they would be in a detailed building cost estimate. The substitution of embodied energy for dollars provides a fine-grain picture of this critical factor. It is possible to estimate the embodied energy in different construction approaches to similar buildings, such as steel frame versus reinforced concrete frame.

Using information from the *Handbook*, several scenarios have been evaluated for building reuse as compared with demolition and replacement. Preserving just the structure and replacing the envelope, mechanical, electrical, and plumbing systems, finishes, and equipment will still save 20 to 30 percent of the embodied energy. Depending on the extent to which existing materials and systems can be reused, this percentage will increase and can approach 100 percent.

Put into units of energy, every square foot of building reused to offset the need for new construction will save the equivalent of somewhere between one and eleven gallons of oil, depending on type of building and the amount of construction required for the upgrade. Various sources estimate the total new building construction in the United States at about four billion square feet per year. If a program

to reuse and recycle our existing building stock were applied to our national construction mix and produced savings averaging just 250,000 Btu per square foot, annual energy savings would equal one quadrillion Btu. This single strategy represents 1 percent of all energy used in the United States. While 1 percent may not at first appear to be significant, it is equivalent to increasing the efficiency of all US transportation by nearly 5 percent.

To reiterate, because of the vast amount of available data, embodied energy is easily applied as a metric for quantified comparison of environmental benefits of building reuse, but it is far from the only area of concern. Tools exist to evaluate the impact of planning and building design on carbon emission, particulate and chemical pollution, water and air, and arable land. The same tools will also quantify the number of jobs created by alternative planning and design strategies. We can make informed planning and design decisions, considering their environmental and economic impact far beyond the boundaries of the projects themselves.

When the *Handbook* was first prepared in 1979–81, it was anticipated that it would serve not only as a reference but also as a framework to organize and make available new data as they became available. Unfortunately, changing attitudes toward energy and the environment in the 1980s prevented this from happening.

The First Law of Thermodynamics, sometimes referred to as the Law of Conservation of Energy, states that within any closed system the quantity of energy will remain constant even if the form of that energy changes.

4.4

Energy Quantity: The First Law of Thermodynamics

Energy is defined as the ability to do work. All units of energy quantity—Btu, kilowatt-hours, joules—are interchangeable. The state or form of a quantity of energy, whether light, kinetic, chemical, potential, or heat, can be changed from one to another without affecting the total amount of that energy. In quantity a kilowatt-hour of light is the same as a kilowatt-hour of heat or a kilowatt-hour of physical work. The First Law of Thermodynamics states that the amount of energy in a closed system cannot change, that energy is neither created nor destroyed. Yet we find ourselves "running out of energy." The problem is that not all energy is of equal quality. (See 4.5, "Energy Quality: The Second Law of Thermodynamics.")

Despite the fact that the First Law presents only a limited part of the overall picture, it is nonetheless useful in evaluating certain effects of planning and design on sustainability and the environment. Units of energy typically take one of two forms. The first, a force–distance relationship, represents what we generally think of as physical work. A joule is the energy (work) necessary to move a resistance of one Newton through one meter. A foot-pound is the energy to raise one pound one foot. Energy is also quantified in thermal terms. A Btu is the energy required to heat one pound of water one degree Fahrenheit. A calorie is the energy required to heat one gram of water one degree Celsius.

While "energy consumption" is actually a measure of energy degradation and is a Second Law phenomenon, the First Law, the concept of conservation of energy, is also relevant to optimizing building construction and operation. All energy introduced into a building for operation or service will remain in that building unless it is transferred or escapes to the outside. However, the eventual form that this energy takes may not be of a useful quality, at least for the purpose originally intended. All energy forms will move toward and eventually become heat. Light will be absorbed by the surfaces it strikes and become heat. Kinetic energy becomes heat energy as an object in motion is slowed by friction. Combustion of fuel transforms chemical energy to heat. "Waste" energy, such as the heat that results from lighting, transportation of people or materials, or other building functions, can be considered a potential resource. However, this heat

energy will only have value if there is an application that can use it at its existing temperature. Heat energy at 80°F can perform space heating but will not be useful for boiling water, let alone creating light.

Explicitly designing systems to capture "waste" energy is referred to as *cogeneration*. The capture of the waste heat from electric generators is the best known application of cogeneration; there are many others. For example, the heating system in most cars captures the heat energy that results from converting the chemical energy in gasoline to kinetic energy. There are also many instances of "de facto cogeneration." For example, the operation of a television, or any electrical device, will result in the introduction of heat. When heat is needed, this is a benefit; however, when cooling is required, it has a negative impact. The management of "waste" heat is an important part of optimizing overall performance.

It is also important to recognize that the "waste" heat from building equipment and occupants is unavoidable and will be counterproductive whenever excessive heat is already present. Minimizing the amount and therefore the negative effects of unwanted heat becomes contingent on avoiding unnecessary use of energy-consuming systems such as lights and motors.

opposite
The Galleria Vittorio Emanuele, Milan, 1864, provides a unique sense of place that requires virtually no energy for its operation and may actually reduce the heating loads on the adjacent buildings.

The Second Law of Thermodynamics addresses the quality or level of energy. It states that within any closed system, the quality of energy will tend to move toward the lowest level of energy within that system. Energy will seek equilibrium.

4.5

Energy Quality: The Second Law of Thermodynamics

In order to raise the quality of a specific quantity of energy, additional energy must be added. The added energy does not increase the quantity of the original energy, nor does it decrease the quantity of the added energy. Rather, the quality of the added energy decreases as it raises the quality of the original energy. The added energy is therefore "lost" as a useful resource.

A corollary is that in order for energy to be applied to useful ends, it must be moving from a higher to a lower level. Regardless of its quantity, energy at or below the level of its surroundings will be of no practical value. (See 4.6, "Utility of Resource: Entropy.")

There is a broader application of the Second Law of Thermodynamics to considerations of sustainability. When the quality of a resource is raised, such as when it is manufactured as part of a building, many other resources will have to be committed. When that high quality resource is abandoned, as when a building is demolished, resources that were added to raise the quality of the raw materials will be lost.

Quality may refer to the form of the energy—light is a higher quality energy form than heat—or it may refer to the level within a particular form—3000-degree heat is of a higher quality than 300-degree heat. The Second Law addresses the behavior of energy quality in several ways. It states that energy will of its own accord always move toward a lower form or lesser quality, and that transforming energy from a lower quality form to a higher one—such as using heat to create electricity—will require the application of additional energy to achieve this increase in quality. The greater the increase in quality, the more outside energy required.

Another corollary is that regardless of the quantity, an energy resource cannot work on a target that is at a higher level than that of the resource or raise the level of any target above that of the resource. For example, a heat source at 150°F may be able to provide vast amounts of domestic hot water but will not be able to boil even a thimbleful of that same water or, for that matter, raise its temperature above 150°F.

This has several very important applications to opti-mizing building performance. To obtain maximum benefit, the use to which a particular unit of energy is put must be as close as possible in quality to that unit of energy. For example, a unit of solar energy captured for daylighting—a high-level use—will be much more beneficial than a unit captured as heat—a low-level use—providing, of course, that the light is needed.

One way of assessing the added environmental benefit from elevated value is to compare a quan-tity of light energy with the amount of heat energy required to produce that amount of light. Consider a fuel-driven generator that powers an electric light-ing system, one that converts the heat of combus-tion to electricity to light. For all practical purposes, Second Law effects limit the conversion of heat to electricity to about 40 percent. In reality, by the time electricity is used for lighting, the quantity of light energy is substantially less than 30 percent of the quantity of heat energy that was introduced at the generator, regardless of whether that heat came from coal, oil, gas, wood, or solar collectors.

The First Law, that energy is neither created nor destroyed, requires that all of the original resource energy remain, even though only a little more than one fourth appears as light. The other three fourths exists, but at a level significantly lower than that of the original resource. This lowering is the result of raising the level of the remaining one fourth, the tar-get. The commitment of these energy resources has significant cost and environmental implications.

While it might be argued that the environmental effects would be neutral if the heat at the generator was captured solar energy, a clean and renewable source, the size of such capture and conversion mechanisms and the resources that must be com-mitted for their construction will create their own environmental issues, especially when compared with simple apertures that admit daylight into buildings. On the other hand, currently, there are no means for the direct storage of light, which means that the direct use of solar energy for lighting is only possible during daylight hours and when weather conditions permit. Still, there are any number of situ-ations where there is abundant daylight available, yet lighting is provided using electricity produced by thermal generators, generally using nonrenew-able and carbon-releasing fuels. This may be seen as an economic or an energy issue, but it also gives tangible form to the inherent logic of direct use of high-quality resource.

The Second Law demonstrates that direct use of an energy resource in its naturally available form will require less of that resource to achieve the same results than will more complicated, indirect systems and will require simpler infrastructure, whether at the scale of building, community, or region. In general, the direct use of resources will create less environmental disruption. For example, a system that uses photovoltaic panels to produce electricity to power fluorescent lamps will need to harvest four to six times as much solar energy as would be needed if solar energy were

used directly as light. Obvious benefits of direct use are that the amount of surface or collection area is far less and that systems are far simpler, reducing the manufacture and cost of material. Direct use also means that less of the sun's energy needs to be intercepted, leaving more for other purposes, such as lighting exterior spaces, growing plants, or perhaps melting snow. While the environmental benefits from having to intercept less of the sun's energy may not be immediately apparent, the impact of the shadows that would be created by large-scale photovoltaic collection can become significant, particularly as they serve areas of high demand. (See 8.8, "Cities, Energy and Architecture.")

All else being equal, the basic planning and design of a building in order to maximize the productive use of daylight will be a far more environmentally sound—and incidentally, cost-effective—energy saving strategy than adding solar electric generation to a building in which daylight is ignored. (See 8.6, "Skylights versus Photovoltaic Panels.")

An architecture that seeks to optimize the direct use of solar energy requires that issues of building configuration, program organization, and envelope performance be addressed as integral elements in the design process. Similarly, the applications of other naturally present resources such as prevailing wind and gravity (or convection) ventilation will inform design. Such consideration is relatively rare in current practice; however, these issues have shaped many of the icons of Modernism.

Further, when considering options for improving the performance of modern-style buildings, these same considerations of direct natural resource application become the initial bases for a comprehensive upgrade.

Another way of envisioning the Second Law effects on the indirect use of solar power is to consider both the processes and scale of hydro or wind generation. In both of these systems, solar energy is the primary driving force and in both cases, the initial event is the transformation of solar energy to heat. Wind results from the differential heating by the sun of various areas of the earth. The energy that drives a hydroelectric generator comes from the potential energy in water at an elevated level. The energy that raised this water was the solar heat that evaporated ocean and surface water, allowing it to rise as a gas and then condense and eventually become rain or snow, which recharged higher elevation lakes, rivers, and reservoirs.

Were it not for the continuing energy from the sun, the winds would slow down and stop as a result of friction—wind resistance between the air and ground and between one part of the air mass and another, the kinetic energy of the moving air becoming heat. Were it not for the continuing energy from the sun, the potential energy of the water in high lakes would degrade as the water flowed to the oceans and, without evaporation, remained there. At first glance, it might seem as though this potential energy is lost—a contradiction to the First Law.

opposite and above

Formwork and reinforcing for the balcony structure at St. Johns Abbey Church in Collegeville, Minnesota prior to the placement of concrete and as completed. Clearly the embodied value of the finished work is far greater than that of the raw materials, 1954–68. Marcel Breuer and Associates (MBA/GPS).

However, closer examination shows that the flow causes the water level in the oceans to rise, albeit minutely, thus increasing the potential energy of the oceans. The problem with this transfer of potential energy from the lakes and rivers to the ocean is that the potential energy of the water added to the oceans is at the same level as oceans themselves, making it unavailable for the performance of useful work. Further, not only has the level of the energy in the water from the lakes and rivers dropped to that of the ocean, the addition of that water has raised the level of the oceans, thereby reducing the differential between the supply and the receiver. (See 4.6, Utility of Resource: Entropy.")

On a global scale, the quantity of energy in wind and rain is immense; however, neither the energy potential in the rain falling on a city nor the wind passing through it will come close to providing the energy needs of contemporary society. Energy must be collected and concentrated. The concentration may be the result of time or space. Nonrenewable fossil fuels are the product of concentration over time, solar energy converted to plant and animal material, transformed over millennia into relatively pure carbon-based fuels. Wind and hydro systems collect and concentrate solar-driven energy by utilizing natural phenomena that occur regardless of whether the energy is eventually captured; however, the amount of energy actually available at the capture point is remarkably little compared to the initial solar energy driving the system. Take, for example, the water that is raised to power the turbines at Grand Coulee, Bonneville, Glen Canyon, and dozens of lesser-known hydroelectric plants along the Columbia, Snake, and Colorado rivers. The plants are primarily driven by the solar energy received across thousands of square miles—hundreds of trillions of square feet—of the Pacific Ocean. A small part of that energy is transformed into increased potential in the water vapor, which eventually becomes clouds above the western mountain ranges. Still less of that energy ends up as precipitation entering the watersheds that feed the lakes and rivers above the dams. Not only is the captured energy a relatively small percentage of the potential energy in the water that evaporates from the oceans, each of the multiple transformations in form and quality of energy—from light to heat, to potential energy at the height of clouds, to potential energy at the height of the reservoirs above the dams and turbines, to the kinetic energy of the water flowing through the turbines, to the kinetic energy from the turbine shaft driving the generator to electric energy—each results in quantitative or First Law "losses," reductions in the amount of energy that can perform useful work. The effect of these losses is that to be meaningful the collection and concentration systems require a scale that has global implications. (See 5.5 "Density of Renewable Energy: Natural Distribution.")

Most of this process is "natural," which is to say that it would occur without human intervention. It is renewable, in that it is driven by the steady flow of energy from the sun. However, it is finite, in that

areas of the planet that form the collection and concentration system are limited. Finally, and perhaps most important, it is not ecologically benign; we have seen intense discussions regarding the environmental impacts of large- and small-scale hydroelectric projects.

Modernism gives us a perspective that brings space and time into the understanding of Second Law behavior, particularly as it applies to issues of sustainability. It also demands the application of resources to relevant needs using the most direct processes. Similarly, consideration of the immense inventory of modern-style buildings, recognizing their value as resource, will lead inevitably to their continued use, an essential component in any comprehensive strategy to achieve sustainability.

Trenton, New Jersey, Integrated Community
Energy System central plant in which waste
heat from electric generation is captured and
used to heat and cool more than thirty buildings.
TSP/Elemental Architecture, 1980.

Entropy is energy at the same level as its surroundings.
As such, it is unavailable for application to useful ends. Within a
closed system, the movement of energy from a higher to lower state
not only reduces the amount of high-level energy, it also raises the
level of the surroundings—increases entropy, thus reducing the
potential value of whatever high-level energy remains.

In broader terms, entropy may describe any condition in which the
value or importance of any resource is determined by its differentiation
from its surroundings. Construction materials manufactured and
assembled as a building become high-value resources. The same
materials in a landfill become an increase in entropy. The homogenization
of the cultural environment, the loss of genius loci, increases cultural
entropy. The loss of environmental diversity increases environmental
entropy.

4.6

Utility of Resource: Entropy

The First Law of Thermodynamics states that energy is neither created nor destroyed, so we do not actually "consume" energy. The Second Law of Thermodynamics states in part that to be useful, energy must be at a higher level than its surroundings and that the level of energy resources effecting work will drop. This leads to two conclusions. First, in order to utilize an energy resource there must be a receiver for this energy, and this receiver must be at a lower state than that of the resource. Second, as the resource is applied and its level falls, it approaches that of the receiver. When the resource and the receiver reach at the same level, the resource has no practical value.

Entropy is a resource at the same level or state as its surroundings, therefore having no utility. While entropy is generally applied to states of energy, it may also refer to virtually any condition of resource. For example, a brick is at a higher state than a pile of clay. For the pile of clay to become a brick, external resources including human labor and heat energy in the kiln must be added. Despite the application of these resources, in the end, the brick itself only possesses the resource of the clay. The quality of

the resources applied to transform the clay to brick decline, and those resources become part of the pool of entropy.

For the understanding of sustainable architecture, this is relevant in that we do not actually create nor destroy resources, at least in a physical sense. We do, however, change them, and in changing them we greatly affect the entropic condition of the earth. When buildings are created, the state of the raw materials that go into their making is raised, but in doing so, the state of the resources that are required for this transformation are lowered, becoming entropy.

When buildings are demolished, the state of the discarded materials drops to that of the material in the landfill. All of the resources that were embodied during the making of the building, energy and others, become entropic; they cannot be reapplied. If these new resources are nonrenewable, they will be exhausted within a relatively short time. If they are renewable, the rate at which they can be accessed is limited. When materials are recycled for reuse in new locations, some of the embodied resources

above and opposite

New York City's original Pennsylvania Station by
McKim, Mead, and White during demolition in 1965.
The embodied value of the scrap steel is a small fraction
of the structure in place and an even smaller fraction of the
building functioning as a primary gateway to New York.

are recovered, offsetting the need to commit new resources; however, the recovered resources are far less than they would be had they been reused in place.

Given the immense global demands, from food and shelter to education, health care, recreation, and cultural and spiritual experience, it should be immediately apparent that the allocation and application of resources is of paramount impor-tance. The consideration of entropy demands that resources be used at their highest possible level. For the built environment, the stock of existing buildings represents resources at a very high state. A Modernist strategy for meeting human needs at this point in time will begin with an investigation of the available building stock. Decisions will be informed by evaluation of the resources that will be required to upgrade this stock as compared with demolition and replacement.

above
Variety, apparently random, within rigid order. Shangai.

opposite
A moment of clarity and poignancy before entropy. Near Lyon.

Thermal mass refers to the amount of thermal energy that a material can absorb per unit of change of temperature. For example, it takes much more energy to heat a pound of water ten degrees than it does to heat a pound of aluminum. A pound of water has a higher thermal mass.

Designs employing thermal mass performance can take maximum advantage of available heat when heat is needed and reduce the need for mechanical cooling when the building would otherwise be too warm. Improper use of thermal mass can slow a building's response to changing temperatures, causing energy waste.

4.7

Thermal Mass

Thermal mass is the capacity of a material or a group of materials to store heat energy per unit of temperature change. For example, one pound of water will rise 1°F when 1 Btu is added. Ten pounds of water will rise 1° F when 10 Btu are added. Ten pounds of water has ten times the thermal mass of one pound of water. One pound of aluminum will rise about 4.65°F when 1 Btu is added; conversely, 0.215 Btu will cause 1 pound of aluminum to rise 1°F. A pound of water can store nearly five times more thermal energy than a pound of aluminum within a given temperature range.

Thermal mass can be controlled by changing the amount of material in a system or the thermal density (specific heat) of the material used. In terms of its relationship to building design, thermal mass will affect the amount of heat that can be stored by the building itself without causing the interior temperature to move outside an acceptable range. It will affect how much heat must be introduced and stored in the building elements in order reach an acceptable level when heating is required, and how much heat must be removed when cooling is required.

There are potential benefits to both low and high thermal mass strategies. A low thermal mass building responds to changing conditions more rapidly and with less added energy. With modern controls and highly responsive heating and cooling systems, a low thermal mass building can accurately track design conditions, avoiding excessive heating and cooling. A high thermal mass building remains at acceptable temperatures for longer periods without having to operate energy-consuming systems; however, it also requires additional heating or cooling once the interior conditions have moved outside the acceptable range.

Generally, there is limited ability to significantly alter the thermal mass of an existing building. However, it remains important to recognize how the thermal mass, high or low, affects the building performance, to take advantage of the benefits that the particular thermal mass condition offers and to mitigate the problems it may create.

The beneficial use of thermal mass can be seen in the case of a high thermal mass building in a climate where the daily temperatures range both

above and below acceptable interior temperatures, hotter during the day and colder at night. An adobe block building in the southwestern United States is a representative example. During the day, when the outside temperatures are hotter than what is desired for the inside, the high thermal mass absorbs large amounts of heat while experiencing a relatively small temperature change. This serves the dual functions of limiting interior temperature increase and storing heat energy. At night, when the outside temperatures drop below acceptable inside levels, the heat stored in the adobe is released. The effect of the thermal mass is to significantly reduce the temperature peaks and valleys. It acts as a thermal flywheel.

Where energy-consuming systems are required, the flywheel effect can also delay the impact of excessive heat loss or gain, reducing peak demand. This reduces the size of the equipment required to maintain acceptable interior temperatures and the size of the service necessary to power these systems. At a larger scale, this strategy allows a smaller utility infrastructure. Similarly, the delay in impact can allow systems to be run during off-peak times so that their operation does not place demands on the utility's least efficient equipment. The benefits are both environmental and economic. (See 5.1, "Energy and Power and Demand.")

High thermal mass can also work against energy efficiency. When the exterior temperature is always either above or below the required inside temperature and interior conditions are adjusted to meet varying needs, such as with nighttime setbacks, the flywheel effect causes the building

to respond more slowly. Consider the simple case of a building envelope with high thermal mass that is occupied eight hours a day, five days a week. In cold seasons, the building and envelope must be heated each morning before the occupants arrive. During this preheat period, the building is at a higher temperature than is needed for its unoccupied state. Although the building can coast for some time at the end of the workday, it can not be allowed to drop to the nighttime setback temperature without causing discomfort. Thus, at the end of the workday, the building is at the lowest temperature acceptable for occupancy but well above acceptable nighttime levels. When the building is coasting down to its nighttime levels, it is at a higher temperature than needed. Since heat loss is in part a function of the temperature difference between inside and out, the heat loss during the extended unoccupied preheat and cool-down periods is greater than what would occur in a building with less thermal mass, which would have faster transitions between occupied and unoccupied temperature.

As is so often the case, there is no single correct approach to the use of thermal mass. Environmental and energy use benefits result from the informed selection of a strategy and then the optimization of that strategy. Understanding the thermal behavior of the given conditions and designing systems and controls to take advantage of these conditions becomes particularly important. (See 7.2, "Envelope and Thermal Mass," and 9.3, "South Jamaica Branch Library.")

opposite
The southeast orientation and the massive thermal flywheel effect of the cliff walls at Canyon de Chelly, New Mexico, dramatically moderate the extreme temperatures characteristic of altitudes above 5,600 feet.

5

Counting Resources

Power is the rate of energy use. It may refer to an actual rate of flow, or it may describe the capacity of a system to deliver or convert energy. *Demand* is the corollary to power. It may describe the actual rate at which a system utilizes energy, or it may describe the maximum rate at which a system might use energy.

Issues of demand and power impact the environment by their effects on the size of infrastructure systems and the degree to which energy needs can be satisfied using the most environmentally responsive equipment.

5.1

Energy/Power and Demand

Energy may be considered "stuff" that has the dimensions of quantity and quality and behaves according to the First and Second Laws of Thermodynamics. Power defines a rate, the rate at which energy is used or the rate at which a system can deliver it. Like energy, issues of power significantly affect the environment, and power considerations play an important role in planning and design. Within a building or community, reduced demand will allow building and local systems to be smaller, with all of the attendant cost and environmental benefits. The effect of reducing building demand on regional and national infrastructure systems will be to reduce the size of those systems and the need to operate the most environmentally damaging components of those systems.

Power may refer to the capacity of an infrastructure system to deliver service. Increasing the size of that system will require the commitment of the materials for fabrication and construction and will impact the land the systems occupy. The energy embodied in the construction of electric and gas utilities represents slightly more than 1 percent of all US energy use. A program to shift energy production

to renewable sources will cause this number to rise dramatically. This is not to say that the shift should not be made, but rather that, from an environmental or energy point of view, it will not come for free.

Power may also be considered from the user side, the demand placed on the infrastructure system. Reducing demand will have multiple benefits. Infrastructure systems can be smaller, with all of the benefits just described. Reduced demand means that as new sources such as wind and photovoltaic generation come on line, they will satisfy a greater percentage of total energy use. (See 5.3, "Incremental Resource Use and the Relationship to Renewables.")

The concept of environmental benefit resulting from decreased demand goes far beyond energy and infrastructure systems. The Earth has only a limited capacity to produce renewable resources. They are renewable only as long as their rate of use does not exceed this capacity. The building construction industry places many demands on the ecosystem, for energy as well as the physical resources of building materials, land, water, and human labor. If needs can be met with less

building, the consumption of nonrenewable and energy-intensive building materials can be reduced, but perhaps more importantly, the rate at which renewable resources are used will be less likely to exceed the Earth's capacity to produce them. The same will result if building construction materials are used more efficiently. As noted earlier, the most efficient use of the construction materials in existing buildings is to reuse those materials in place.

We are at the earliest stages of a massive transition from nonrenewable to renewable energy sources. This is not a matter of choice. The time frame for exhausting the Earth's fossil fuel resources is very short, regardless of which estimates are used. The transition will place a tremendous demand on the total production capacity of our country and of the world. It will require vast new production and generation facilities, and it will mean significant changes in how energy is distributed. To the extent that the demand for these new energy forms can be controlled, the scale of the associated infrastructure can be limited. Limiting the size of new infrastructure components will free up capacity for other vital work, including shelter, education, and health care.

The relationship between new infrastructure and the existing built environment is twofold. Although we cannot afford to have inefficient buildings, total replacement of our building stock would require that building construction alone receive the equivalent of one to two years of all national energy consumption. If this were to happen over a ten-year

period, 10–20 percent of all national energy use would have to be diverted to building construction. This would have a profound effect on energy use and delivery, and the impact on supply of basic materials such as steel and concrete would affect highways, rail systems, and even the creation of new, renewable energy systems. Construction capacity is limited and must be carefully allocated. This is a question of demand.

We need new buildings and we need new infrastructure—transportation and energy systems. It is clear, however, that the rate at which these can be implemented is constrained by the physical limits of the planet. Whenever an existing building can be upgraded, rather than demolished and replaced, the demand for energy and other resources used for construction is reduced. Whenever we improve the performance of an existing building, we not only reduce the use of resources for operation, we also reduce the need to enlarge all of the systems— energy, water, sewer—that serve the building and its community.

Resources not committed to building construction and operation can be applied to other uses. Overall reduction in resource consumption allows a greater portion of all supplies to come from sustainable sources. Reduced demand means smaller infrastructure systems with all of the benefits that this entails, including the possibility of creating smarter, more reliable systems at a faster rate and a lower cost.

Engine hall at Trenton Integrated Community Energy System central plant, viewed from visitors' gallery. TSP/Elemental Architecture, 1980.

The point at which energy, other resource usage, or environmental impact is measured will produce very different quantitative results. Each will offer understanding of different sets of conditions.

5.2

End Use versus Source

Inevitably, committing resources at a building or at a construction site triggers the commitment of the many additional resources needed to process and deliver the original resources to the point of use. The immediate and direct results of architectural decisions will affect the demand created at the building or construction site border; however, the secondary impacts will extend throughout the economic and production chains, back to the initial extraction and processing of raw materials. Architects do not, in general, design the processes that produce the resources and materials used by and for their buildings, but an appreciation of levels of sustainability among alternative measures will inform design approaches, particularly when these alternatives have substantially different environmental impacts. For both construction and building operation, these impacts can be analyzed at a number of different points, each offering different but meaningful information.

In order to understand the implications of a set of data, it must be placed into context. For example, energy data concerning heating a building may be describing conditions occurring anywhere along the entire process, from the escape of heat from the building at one end to the initial extraction of the raw energy resources at the other. The relevance and meaning of the information will be very different depending on where data is taken. The heat loss from the building less the internal heat gains from occupants and energy-consuming equipment within the space and solar heat gain will be the load on the heating system. Information on heat loss will describe the performance of the envelope and be an important part of any strategy for minimizing energy use for space heating. However, it does not, in itself, quantify the environmental effect of the process except for the very small extent to which building heat loss increases global entropy.

Another point in the process for evaluation is the delivery of heat to the space or spaces that are being conditioned. In order to maintain a constant temperature, this will equal the heat loss less the internal and solar gains. While this may seem obvious, consideration of the dynamic interrelationships of the three aspects—heat loss, heat gains, and heat from the heating system—will suggest the demands on, and therefore the design of, the

heating supply and control systems. The design of an appropriate system must consider the dynamic conditions as well as the peak requirements.

The output of the building's primary heating equipment—boiler, furnace, heat pump—will be essentially the same as heat delivered to the spaces plus any losses to the outside, such as from pipes or ducts in unheated crawlspaces or shafts. These points of measurement and analysis are relevant to building design and building efficiency but do not, in themselves, address environmental effect.

Operating heating equipment will create a demand for energy resources, either fuel or electricity. The demand for resources will be determined by the demand for heat and the efficiency of the building equipment in utilizing the resource. In the case of heating equipment, it is important to be clear: are the energy resources being converted into heat or are they being used to raise the level of some other source of heat? Conversion of resource to heat occurs directly in the burning of fuels such as oil or gas or indirectly in the use of electric resistance heating. Use of energy to change the quality of an already existing heat source to a useful level occurs in the case of a heat pump, which raises the temperature of an ambient heat source, such as the outside air or groundwater, whether it is below the ground, or surface water such as a lake.

Finally, the measurement of the demand for energy at the building perimeter, whether by simulation during the design phase or by metering an operating building, defines the effect the demand that the building has on the infrastructure systems that serve it. This is generally considered the end use and is often quantified as total Btu per square foot. Being strictly quantitative and equating all forms of energy including fuel and electricity, it is a First Law view. While end-use performance may be useful in comparing one building to another, it ignores the effects upstream of the building perimeter. Depending on the efficiency of the infrastructure system, equal units of two different energy forms may have profoundly different environmental costs, the Second Law.

To the infrastructure system, the building is the end user, just as the heat loss from the building is the end user of the building system. Knowing the use of energy at the building, and at all other end users, will inform the design of the infrastructure but will still not, in itself, quantify environmental impact. Each component of infrastructure, whether the electric utility or the oil industry, has its own levels of First Law efficiency; that is, the quantity of energy delivered divided by the total quantity of energy resource required for production and delivery. In general, higher levels of delivered energy will require the commitment of more total energy than lower levels. The differences in First Law efficiency among energy delivery systems are significant. One hundred units of energy delivered to the building as fuel oil will require about 110 units of source energy. One hundred units of energy delivered

to the building as electricity will require about 350 units of source energy.

The increased source energy needed to create electricity results in a product at a very high level compared to heat. Either electricity or direct combustion of fuel may be used to generate heat in a building but, considering the efficient use of fuel resources, electricity should rarely be used where fuel can be used directly. (See 5.3, "Incremental Resource Use and the Relationship to Renewables.")

As with virtually every aspect of sustainable design, absolute statements are few and far between. For example, kerosene can be used directly for lighting in gas mantle lamps. The problem is that the efficiency of light production from burning gas is very low, so that even with the significant losses associated with the production and distribution of electricity, burning fuel directly for light is still dramatically less efficient than electric lighting. A complete picture of the environmental impact of planning, construction, and building operation alternatives will require the examination of resource commitment at all points along the various processes. (See 8.7, "Kerosene–Electric Lighting Comparison.")

Evaluation of end use, source, and intermediate conditions will each provide important albeit incomplete information to support planning and design decisions; however, to be meaningful the implications of each data set must be well understood.

Energy resources in similar forms are largely interchangeable. This is particularly true of grid-connected electric generation in which all electricity is fed into a common distribution system. There is no way to identify the original source of any unit of energy consumed. In an interconnected system run for environmental benefit, any reduction in usage, whether from conventional or "green" sources, can decrease demand on the most damaging sources.

5.3

Incremental Resource Use and the Relationship to Renewables

This argument is often heard: As long as energy, or for that matter any resource, is coming from renewable sources, its use does not compromise sustainability, and therefore we do not need to consider the efficiency with which we use it. This is a serious miscomprehension. For the foreseeable future, the primary sources for a significant portion of our energy will be nonrenewable and carbon-based. With increasing global interconnection and interchangeability, a change in demand in one place will be felt everywhere. If renewable energy is collected and used locally, that locality will impose a reduced demand on the greater infrastructure. The more efficiently that renewable energy is used, the greater the reduction in demand for energy from nonrenewable sources. The impact of replacing carbon-based fuels with non-carbon resources will have a similar global scope.

Similarly, one often hears that evaluations of oil savings resulting from a reduction in electric usage should consider the overall mix of primary energy sources used in producing electricity—coal, oil, natural gas, nuclear, hydro, wind, photovoltaic—and prorate the savings among all of those primary resources. This too is wrong. Utilities generally operate on the basis of "economic dispatch." That is, they run the most economical generators to provide their base load requirements and add gen-

erating capacity to meet intermittent demand using the most cost-efficient generators available at each step in the process. If, instead of looking at the monetary cost, environmental economy becomes the basis for "economic dispatch," any reduction in electric use will reduce the operation of the most environmentally damaging generating source.

The concept of incremental use applies equally well to other resources of limited availability. For example, saving a gallon of oil can offset the need to obtain new oil from some particularly environmentally sensitive area such as the Arctic National Wildlife Refuge or politically sensitive area such as the Middle East, even if the oil in question happens at the moment to be coming from Louisiana. In the case of renewable resources that are limited in rate of supply or capacity, a reduction in demand for one use will free up capacity in another.

It is certain that we will be relying on petroleum as a major primary energy source for at least this and the next generation. It is also certain that carbon-based energy sources will be required to supply a significant portion of our needs for the foreseeable future. Any savings that we are able to achieve will allow reduction in the use of our scarcest and most environmentally damaging energy forms.

Renewable resource utilization is not environmentally neutral. The manufacture of the equipment to capture these resources is resource-intensive. The installation and operation of systems for harvesting renewable resources affects ecosystems. The effects of modifying large areas of the natural environment are not well understood.

5.4

Renewable Resources: Effect on the Environment

Renewable is not the same as *infinite* except, perhaps, in the time dimension. While there is a constant flow of solar energy to earth, there is a finite quantity reaching the earth's surface in any given time. Currently, we are using a relatively small percentage of this total solar energy; however, even now we see the effects of the competition among solar-based resources, most dramatically in the case of food and biofuels. This should come as no surprise. The production of food is essentially dependent on the bioconversion of solar energy through photosynthesis. This includes the direct consumption of plant matter and the consumption of animal product which is, in turn, dependent on plants for food.

The 1972 book *The Limits to Growth* modeled several scenarios in which per-capita food supply peaked and then fell sharply early in the twenty-first century. Although dire in their projections, these models did not account for the accelerating effect created by large-scale biofuel production which exacerbated the problem. In 1993, I wrote in *Energy Conscious Architecture* that "If we were to cultivate biofuels, we would have to consider the consequences of trade-offs with competing, cultivated products such as food, cloth fibers, etc." It is not that either the authors of *The Limits to Growth* or I had magical foresight, but rather that the conditions of finiteness and the inevitable effects of approaching the absolute limits of availability of essential resources were obvious, once one took the time to think about them.

We can, with a high degree of accuracy, quantify our renewable resources. Given the growth rates in demand, this analysis should be profoundly sobering. The need to make best use of these precious resources should be immediately apparent. The analytic aspects of Modern practice and design will be at the heart of any meaningful reformulation of our profession.

Two concepts of "car" (1973).

The density of solar energy reaching the earth's surface (insolation) is very low compared to contemporary urban or manufacturing demands. This is dramatically demonstrated by the scale of the natural processes that concentrate and store the effects of insolation.

5.5

Density of Renewable Energy: Natural Distribution

The availability of solar energy, that seemingly endless renewable resource, is in fact limited by the rate at which it arrives at the Earth's surface. The availability of useful energy derived from solar sources is further limited by the efficiency (or inefficiency) of conversion. In practical terms, there are several ways to quantify this.

The annual solar energy striking the ground in New York City is approximately 450,000 Btu per square foot, about 130 kWhr per square foot. If this energy could all be captured and stored to be consumed by a commercial building that is in use for 3,120 hours per year (10 hours per day, six days per week), this would provide about .04 kW, or 40 Watts, per square foot *of building footprint*. But since most buildings are not single story, this energy must be distributed among the multiple floors. For a simple ten-story building, the total annual solar energy arriving at the portion of the earth's surface covered by the building averages to 4 Watts per square foot of floor area. However, this analysis has not considered the efficiency factors for collection, storage, and distribution. While photovoltaic collection efficiencies approaching 50 percent have been reached in pro-

totypes, an overall efficiency of 25 percent, including storage, and conversion, would be a much more realistic figure. In other words, if a ten-story building had solar collectors equal to its entire footprint and collected and stored solar energy whenever it was available, it would only capture enough energy to provide an average of about one Watt per square foot while that building was in operation. This is far less than even a very highly efficient commercial building consumes. For example, a building using 35,000 Btu per square foot per year at the building perimeter and operating 3,120 hours per year would be using more than three Watts per square foot.

It is tempting to think about the vertical surfaces of the building as a means of increasing collection surface. While this is an option for a stand-alone building, as density increases buildings quickly begin to shade one another. Ultimately, there is only a finite amount of solar energy reaching the Earth's surface. This is apparent in an analysis included in a 2006 essay written for the 150th anniversary of the founding of the American Institute of Architects, which looks at the solar potential of a typical 200-by-1000 foot New York City block. The essay's conclu-

sion is similar: A contemporary, efficient, dense urban development cannot be energy independent using the solar energy within its own boundaries. (See 8.8, "Cities, Energy, and Architecture.")

Urban buildings cannot be self-sufficient based on solar power, yet urban conditions have proved to offer the most energy-efficient living situations, providing tremendous cultural and economic benefits. In order for cities to exist, they must draw on outlying areas for energy as well as other essentials, including water, food, and waste disposal. But this does not mean that cities are parasites. Cities provide services and experiences that demand the density that only they can offer. Further, if the all of the activities that occur in our cities were instead distributed in a low-rise, automobile-dependent configuration, there would not only be a dramatic increase in resource consumption but also a massive loss of open space.

In fact, the relationship between cities and their surroundings is highly symbiotic—connected and interdependent. If we are to address the vast range of problems associated with limited resource availability and environmental degradation, first order considerations will be at the broad, societal level. Even when designing individual buildings we must recognize that each building type imposes its own restrictions on regional planning alternatives and that there are substantial differences among the associated effects on the ecosystem that result from these restrictions. There is no gain in produc-

ing environmentally efficient buildings if they force land-use patterns that are inherently wasteful of the very resources the individual buildings are conserving. The striking, although not particularly surprising, conclusion is that an environmentally sustainable existence employing and offering contemporary practices relies on interconnectedness and cooperation. We must think holistically.

Understanding the processes of resource utilization is an underlying precondition for making informed choices. Solar energy is the most obvious and by far the greatest source of renewable energy. Not only can it be used directly for light and heat, captured and stored as heat and electricity, it is also the prime energy source for wind and hydro power, both of which can be converted to electricity through the use of turbines.

The following offers geographical scale to the Second Law discussion of hydro power in section 4.5. The processes that enable hydroelectric generation start with energy from the sun striking the surface of the earth. Water, whether in oceans or lakes or as moisture on the ground, is warmed and evaporates. The water vapor rises, partly as a result of its own buoyancy and partly as a result of the rising air currents that are also driven by solar energy. In the colder upper air, the water vapor condenses to become clouds, which may be anywhere from 2,000 to 25,000 feet above the sea level. The potential energy of the water, as with any mass, increases with height, an increase that must come from some outside source, in this case the sun. The moisture in

the clouds becomes precipitation and falls to earth, often at a level high above sea level; however, the loss in elevation between the cloud and the ground will result in a loss of potential energy. In the case of hydroelectric sites, the precipitation within the catchment area flows to a collection point—a lake or reservoir. The additional drop in elevation from the initial impact point to the reservoir's surface produces an additional loss of potential energy.

The driving force for hydroelectric generation is the potential energy of the water due to its height above the level of the turbines. This is, generally speaking, the height of the dam creating the reservoir. Once the water leaves the turbine and continues its passage toward the sea, it will continue to lose potential energy, none of which is captured for human use. It is, of course, possible to have a series of reservoirs and dams at successively lower levels capturing additional energy along the way, but in each case, the useful potential energy will be limited to the height of the water in the reservoir above the level of the turbine. The points in the overall cycle of the solar-driven water—from the sea to clouds to rain to rivers and lakes and back to the sea—where useful energy is extracted are very limited.

The general case is interesting; however, a specific example is eye-opening. The Grand Coulee Dam is the largest hydroelectric facility in the United States and the fourth largest in the world. The water level at the top of the dam is 1,311 feet above sea level; its hydraulic height (the height of the water above the

turbine outlets) is given as 380 feet. In other words, of the potential energy that was obtained from solar energy, which raised the water to become clouds at heights ranging from 2,000 to 25,000 thousand feet, only the portion that provided the 380-foot lift is recaptured at the dam. Many points within the catchment area are at elevations well above 3,500 feet. As the water flows from these points to Lake Roosevelt at 1,311 feet, it loses well over half the potential energy it possessed as rain or snow when as it first returned to the earth's surface.

Still, since the receiving area for the solar energy that produces the precipitation that drives the Grand Coulee power plant is immense, that is, the Pacific Ocean, it is reasonable to ask whether the collection inefficiency is meaningful. Further, because the vast collection area serving the Grand Coulee Dam is the natural topography of the northwestern United States and southwestern Canada, the question arises whether the exploitation of this collection and concentration system has any bearing on issues of sustainability. The scale of natural systems compared with current energy usage shows how critical the relationships are.

The catchment area, the collection and concentration system for the Grand Coulee Dam, is reported by the U.S. Department of the Interior as 74,100 square miles. According to the U.S. Energy Information Administration (EIA), the Grand Coulee Dam's hydroelectric capacity is 6,810 megawatts meaning that about 10.9 square miles of catchment

area are needed to support one megawatt of generating capacity. To place this in a larger perspective, the 74,100 square miles is 2.6 percent of the land area of the contiguous 48 states, yet the 6,810 megawatts of the Grand Coulee facility represents only about 0.63 percent of all U.S. electrical generating capacity, 1,087,790 megawatts. This looks at power or capacity. The numbers for the actual energy produced are similar. In 2007, the total electricity produced in the United States was 4.16 trillion kilowatt-hours, again according to the EIA. The average annual production from the Grand Coulee Dam generators was about 21 billion kilowatt-hours, roughly 0.5 percent of the total. (See 5.1, "Energy/Power and Demand.") If the topography and weather patterns of the entire United States were as well suited to hydroelectric production as the Pacific Northwest, which they are not, a hydroelectric system covering the entire land mass of the 48 contiguous states would produce only about one-fifth of our current electric energy needs.

As an order-of-magnitude check on these numbers, the capacities of all of the hydroelectric plants on the Columbia River system above, below, and including the Grand Coulee Dam is 24,150 megawatts. The total catchment area is 260,000 square miles. The ratio of capacity to catchment area for the entire system is 10.8 square miles of catchment area per megawatt of capacity, very similar to that of the Grand Coulee facility itself.

While the numbers are not, in themselves, particularly important to the discussion of sustainable design, the broader conclusion is critical. Solar energy, although renewable, is very diffuse when compared with the intensity of contemporary energy demand. The rate of potential solar capture is limited, and that limit is as significant as those that apply to nonrenewable resources. An oft-used example is that solar energy represents a guaranteed but finite income, while fossil fuels are our savings, amassed over tens and hundreds of millions of years. If we do not live within this finite income, we will have to draw down our savings, and we cannot live indefinitely on these savings.

This is in no way an argument against the use of renewable energy in all of its forms but rather an insistence that all resources, renewable and nonrenewable, are finite, at least to the rate at which they become available, and must be used with great care to optimize benefits. Without this understanding, we will be no better off with regard to exhausting the planet's capacity to provide a steady flow of energy than we have been in consuming its stored fossil fuels. Modernism offers tools for evaluating quantitative factors such as energy consumption and square feet of building construction together with qualitative issues such as preservation of scenic land and human satisfaction.

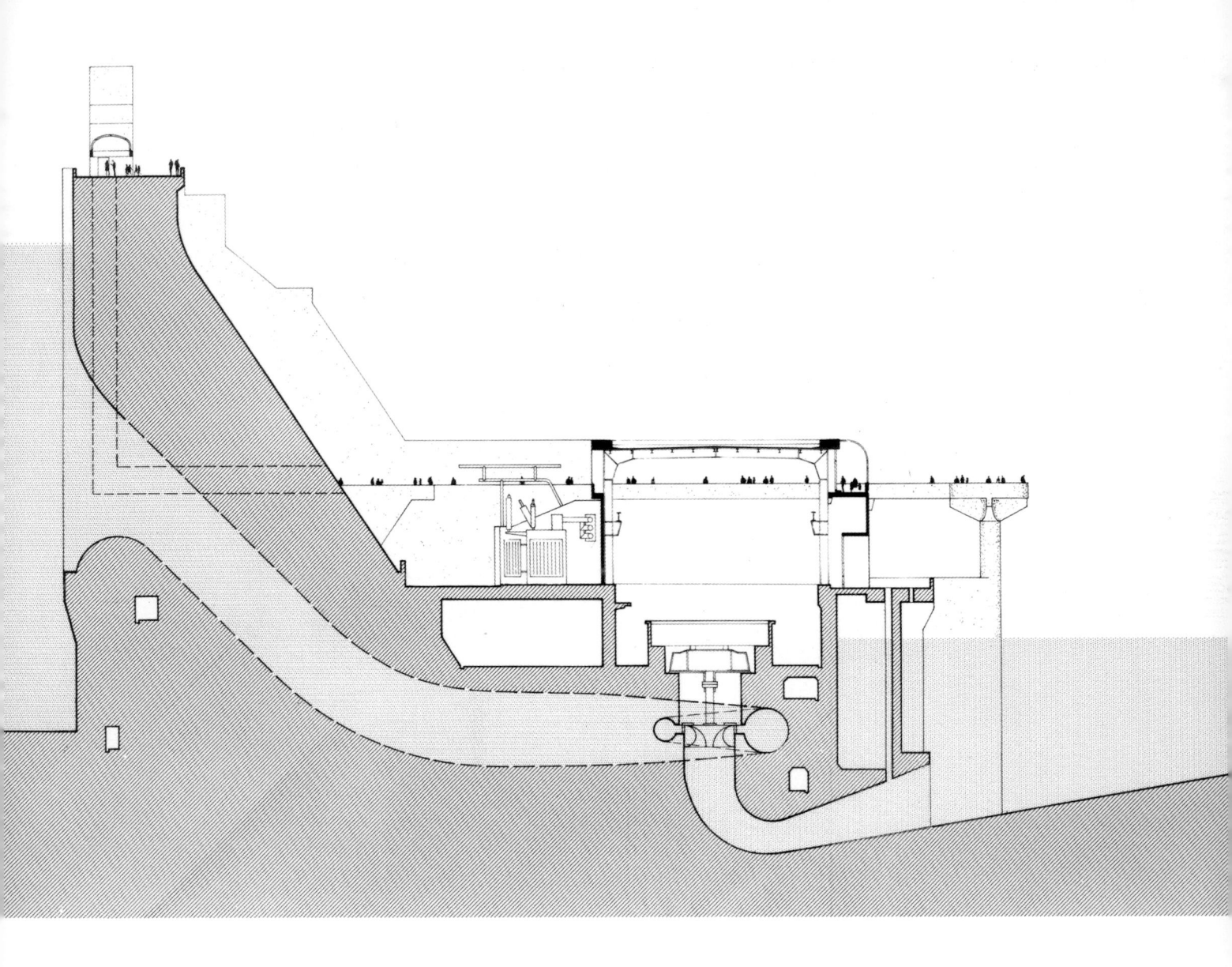

opposite
The Russel Dam and part of the vast reservoir which feeds it. Gatje Papachristou Smith, 1983 (MBA/GPS).

above
Section through Russel Dam. The hydraulic height is the difference in water level between the reservoir at the far left and the receiving pond on the right. Compare this with the change in height of water vapor as it moves from sea level to the clouds. Gatje Papachristou Smith, 1983 (MBA/GPS).

The ability of the planet to process waste is a finite resource, and is holistically interconnected to all other resource usage within the ecosystem.

5.6

Waste Management

The capacity to process and dispose of waste is a finite resource; one that, depending on conditions, may be either renewable or nonrenewable. Some waste products will remain problematic for a period of time sufficiently long that they may be considered permanent. Others wastes may be considered temporary, breaking down relatively quickly through natural processes. Waste takes many forms, including the discarded materials of our daily lives, the sewage that leaves our buildings, the chemical and particulate emissions from fuel-burning engines, the spent fuel from nuclear reactors. It also includes the "waste" heat produced by everything from internal combustion engines to lights and computers.

On a sparsely populated planet, natural processes such as filtration, chemical reaction, photosynthesis, and re-radiation of energy to outer space can process many of these waste products at a rate sufficient to prevent their becoming a problem. This waste processing capacity is a renewable resource, but as with any renewable resource, it is limited in rate, in how much can be handled in any given

time period. As long as the rate of waste discharge is within the capacity of the ecosystem to process it, it does not represent a problem. From the outset of life on this planet, there has been continuous production of materials that we consider waste or pollution, such as carbon dioxide. For most of the earth's history, this has been transformed through natural processes, such as plant growth, which absorbs carbon dioxide and releases oxygen, allowing the environment to remain generally stable. With the increase in human population and the rapid advancement in technology, the rate of our waste discharge has rapidly grown beyond the processing capacity of the ecosystem, with severe and potentially catastrophic results.

There is also waste whose processing is nonrenewable. For example, space required for the disposal of nonbiodegradable waste competes with all other space requirements and limits on space, at least on the planet, are absolute. We have already seen situations in which cities have completely run out of space for landfill. These urban settlements are the most extreme conditions, since their density

produces the greatest amount of waste per unit of land area and the demand for land is most intense. Still, as we have repeatedly seen, once limits are reached in one area, it does not take long for the effects to spread outward.

Proposals have been made to launch waste into outer space or send it to the sun, effectively opening up the earth's closed system and expanding its limits. In addition to the ethical question of whether we should burden the rest of the universe with our problems, the process of transporting the materials has its own set of environmental issues. It seems unlikely that either an environmental or economic analysis could justify the costs of this approach for low-level waste. High-level waste, such as spent radioactive fuel, tends to be extremely dangerous if mishandled. The question of both feasibility and cost of adequate safeguards would certainly impose major added burdens on any program.

Humankind will, of course, continue to produce waste, and an underlying premise of this book is that the human species will survive. This, in turn, demands recognition that waste processing, like the application of every resource, whether renewable or not, must be subject to a comprehensive planning process that considers the ecosystem holistically.

An often-heard statement—that waste is simply a resource that has not been properly utilized— is highly misleading in that it largely ignores the issues of the Second Law and entropy. Whether considering environmental, energy, or economic costs, most of the value embodied in the things that we use and then discard comes from the changes that were made to the basic materials used in their production. When recycled as "raw material," waste retains little of that value. Reuse continues the meaningful application of the resources that were initially committed to create the product in question.

In the case of buildings, the smart reuse of our building stock will satisfy much of our need for built space by using high-quality resources in their highest state. This not only avoids the creation of the waste materials resulting from demolition, it also eliminates the waste inherent in the processes of new building construction.

In Amsterdam, two sides of waste management – a barge load of demolition debris next to masonry building walls in the process of being reused.

6

Process—General

A Modernist approach to sustainability in contemporary architecture will be based on establishing building requirements to meet a set of stated criteria. A design process that satisfies these requirements without excess will avoid casual and wasteful expenditure of scarce resources. Once the outlines of a solution have been established, the components may be optimized. The goal is a solution that serves human needs with minimum damage to the ecosystem. It is not necessarily the design of the greenest building.

This approach should not be confused with minimalism, but rather be seen as appropriate design that, in addition to the environmental benefits, offers much closer contact to authentic conditions and experiences.

6.1

Approaching Sustainability

The greening process will begin with an understanding of the meaning of sustainability as applied to architecture and the creation of a basis for its measurement. Performance evaluation must correlate the delivery of an architectural goal against the environmental cost of achieving that goal. Environmental cost may be defined in many ways. These range from easily quantifiable factors such as energy or water use, carbon release, or land coverage to qualitative concerns such as preservation of historic artifacts or scenic natural sites. A comprehensive view of the environment will include some measure of many of these considerations. Traditionally, architectural goals have been measured in terms of built space. The result is that energy performance is typically defined as Btu per square foot, lighting budgets defined as Watts per square foot, and so forth. Recognizing that resources are finite demands a new criterion for quantifying the product of architecture. Architects must consider the efficacy of their work in meeting needs—human, societal, and global. This not a new idea. In *Energy Conscious Architecture* (1993) I wrote:

We must be clear about the architect's function It is not the primary purpose of architecture to save energy. After all, any building activity, by definition, requires the use of energy. It is, however, the responsibility of architects to carry out their work in a way that gains maximum results from the expenditure of precious nonrenewable resources.

In terms of energy use, the important consideration is not the absolute energy performance of the building as an object but rather its efficiency in meeting a programmatic goal with minimum energy consumption. The same may be said for all aspects of sustainable design. In fact, the interconnectedness of the many aspects of green design will in most cases result in designs in which none of the individual parts is environmentally optimal when viewed in isolation, but which will yield an integrated holistic solution in harmony with the planet.

Just as energy efficiency should not be measured in Btu per square foot but rather in Btu per programmatic goal solution, environmental impact—whether carbon footprint, water consumption, land occupation, use of nonrenewable materials—should not be evaluated per unit of building but instead as it relates to satisfying human needs. This definition of sustainable design requires, in turn, a clarification of what is meant by human needs.

To have a sustainable Modern architecture, it is essential to recognize that human needs supported by that architecture go far beyond the simple issues of shelter or utility. Architecture has the power to create spaces that calm or excite; that focus or expand fields of vision—literal and metaphorical; that offer intellectual clarity or pose demanding questions. Architecture can speak of privacy or community. It can profoundly impact the body, mind, and spirit. Success in addressing all of these issues must be taken into account when assessing the value obtained from the expenditure of environmental capital. (See 3.3, "Modernism and Sustainability.")

Such an architecture requires that architecture itself be re-envisioned. All too often architecture is viewed as object-making, and increasingly, to the degradation of the practice, as simply object-decorating. While each of these endeavors comprises an aspect of the process, the creation of meaningful architecture is, or should be, the comprehensive orchestration of the vast physical resources available to meet out highest needs.

Architecture that addresses programmatic needs is frequently characterized as being more mundane and less creative, less artistic than architecture of pure form. Implied is that useful works constitute a lesser quality of architecture and yield a lesser quality of life. Nothing could be farther from the truth. Architecture, like all art, cannot exist in the absence of or detachment from its interaction with people and context. Human involvement and response—intellectual, emotional, visceral—are essential to the inherent meaning of a work of art. The understanding and appreciation of a building may result as much from the experiences of approach or of controlled views as from the actual forms of the building and spaces they make. Achieving these benefits does not require additional building but rather informed design. Attention is away from rather than toward the building itself. The making of architecture that incorporates human interaction as an intrinsic resource should not be

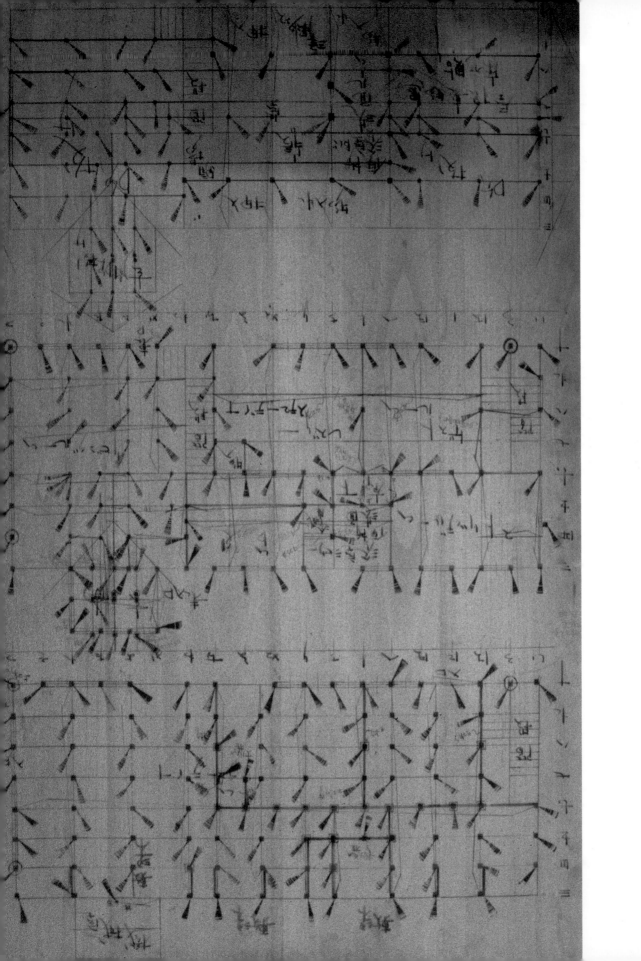

above and opposite

Main components of two of the primary beam connections. Note the relationship between the objects and the means used to describe them.

floor dimensions (space between columns or structural walls). It may also include descriptive aspects (whether wall or column supports are used, or whether the floor system is a flat, ribbed, or waffle slab, planks, or steel deck on beams or joists).

Quantitative items provide an order-of-magnitude check on the capacity of a building to support a particular program, that is, whether the building is generally the right size. However, even if it is not, its use should not be rejected out of hand. A building that is too small may accommodate a portion of a program while a building that is too large may be used by the program in question plus some other use. While this may seem obvious, there have been far too many cases in which a perfectly serviceable structure has been demolished because it was seen as being the wrong size for its intended use.

The descriptive items indicate the relative ease of inserting the specific program spaces into the building as well as the ease with which the primary building elements may be modified to interconnect spaces, either horizontally or vertically.

In order to match building characteristics with programmatic needs, the program must eventually be expressed in terms that coincide with building descriptors—square feet of floor area, volume, and so forth. This, however, is already a shift away from the essence of program, the support of human activity. For example, an office for one person might be a comfortable chair from which the user could run his or her wireless devices. It might be a small enclosed space to allow confidential phone conversations or private meetings with one or two other people, or it might be a larger space for group meetings, personal files, and reference material. It might be a grand space to communicate status or power. Each of these alternatives represents a very different human activity, a different understanding of "office." Meaningful environmental evaluation requires the comparison of ecological costs against activities rather than against some unit of building size.

Thinking of sustainability in terms of the efficiency of providing program or service opens a vast new array of solutions to many of the resource problems that we currently face. It also suggests a view of architecture significantly different from that generally held. Whereas architecture has, in large part, been considered to be object-making, it now becomes the art of meeting human needs through the built environment. The efficiency with which this art is carried out is the measure of its sustainability, a new paradigm.

Traditionally, the units that quantify the factors used to evaluate building performance, such as building size and energy consumption, have been straightforward and easily understood. The new paradigm imposes factors that are more difficult to quantify, such as meeting human needs and environmental cost, yet it is only through the measured consideration of the relationships among these

factors that a truly sustainable architecture will emerge.

In *Towards a New Architecture*, Le Corbusier observed that residential architecture of the time failed to address either the new technologies or the new social patterns. As cited above in 3.2, he wrote:

You employ stone, wood and concrete, and with these materials you build houses and palaces. That is construction. Ingenuity is at work.

He went on to say:

The problem of the house has not yet been stated.

Today, the same might be said regarding sustainability. There are many ways in which we can continue to exist on this planet. Some of these involve the application of technology and technique with the singular goal of reducing environmental degradation, critical but not all-encompassing. There are also approaches that depend on creating a closer bond between humankind and the rest of the earth's ecosystem. This not only offers pragmatic, quantifiable benefits but also allows us to connect emotionally and intellectually with our environments, both natural and cultural. The transcendental experience that arises from such understanding is the art of sustainable design.

The problem of sustainability has not yet been stated.

The building envelope will generally offer the greatest potential for physical change to optimize environmental performance; however, as with all aspects of building design, envelope considerations must not be taken in isolation but be evaluated concurrently with such issues as program, mechanical and electrical systems, and scheduling.

6.4

Envelope: An Introduction

If the first action in the sustainable building reuse is to match a need with a structure, the next step is to review the envelope, what exists and what can be done to improve its performance. The envelope, the interface between inside and out, is simultaneously the primary modifier of harsh exterior conditions, the transmitter and controller of desired aspects of the climate, the means by which building users connect with or are separated from the outside, and the part of the building most people recognize as the building itself. The "inside" created by the envelope is the space controlled by the building—temperature, air, light, security, privacy—and "outside" is everything else. Of course, the boundary is not absolute, nor does it occur at a single point or plane. A porch may provide protection from rain and sun without offering privacy or security. This ambiguity of position—interior or exterior—contributes to the experience of a user of the building, and may also significantly impact dynamic performance. For example, external shading devices that moderate the impact of the sun—brise soleils, louvers, traditional and rolling shutters—create a zone outside what is normally considered the building envelope. This zone, in one sense, becomes the microclimate

"seen" by the building wall at its inner edge and, at the same time, an integral part of the building envelope.

Similarly, devices that redirect or diffuse the sun—light shelves and filters—to improve its usefulness within the building modify how the interior "sees" such external environmental conditions. Elements on the interior—opaque and translucent window coverings, shutters, louvered blinds, movable insulation, interior light shelves—are also envelope components, modifying the interactions between the outside world and the interior environment. The envelope is not a single plane but rather a transitional zone. Physically, it may be compressed into a thin membrane, a glass wall, or it may have significant dimension, a brise soleil facade or a heavy masonry wall. It may also involve several layers as with double skin buildings, some of which may include thermal mass between the inner and outer skin. (See 4.7, "Thermal Mass.")

From a quantitative perspective, the advantage of taking the envelope as the starting point for the consideration of energy consumption is that the

San Francisco de Asis,
Ranchos de Taos, New Mexico,
1772–1816.

Detail of "Cliff Palace" at Mesa
Verde, Colorado, ca. 1190–1260.

The envelope and its components are the primary elements
that define how a building is perceived. The interactions
with sunlight create dynamic sculpture and drama with
minimum demands on the natural environment.

improvement in overall performance resulting from an envelope upgrade requires little or no operating energy. Perhaps a more important reason to begin with the envelope is that the interaction between the environmental context and the building interior directly affects the essential qualities of architectural space. This is a design resource that can be captured with minimal commitment of physical resources, and one that will not result from the use of mechanical systems.

When the building skin interacts with the sun, the occupant senses the potency of solar energy, for better or for worse. This conveys intellectual and visceral understandings of a key renewable energy. It also contributes to an emotional and intuitive reconnection with the natural environment. Conversely, but equally powerful as emotive design, is the awareness of intentional separation such as that created by the sense of comfort experienced when standing inside a high-performance glass curtain wall in the midst of a snowstorm. To quote again from *Towards a New Architecture*

But suddenly you touch my heart, you do me good, I am happy and I say: "This is beautiful." That is Architecture. Art enters in.

above and opposite
Notre-Dame du Haut, Ronchamp, France.
Le Corbusier, 1954.

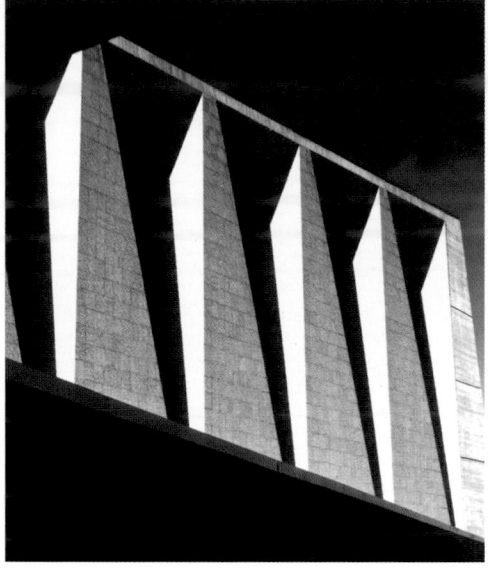

opposite

Bell banner at the Annunciation Priory, Bismark, North Dakota, Marcel Breuer and Associates, 1954–63 (MBA/GPS).

above

Folded concrete plate wall (left) and bell banner and solar reflector (right) at the St. Johns Abbey Church, Collegeville, Minnesota, Marcel Breuer and Associates, 1954–68 (MBA/GPS).

Measuring the environmental performance of the building envelope requires the evaluation of both quantifiable performance and qualitative considerations for each component of the envelope against the effects the resulting selections place on the environment. Unlike pure energy calculations, the units of measurement for the various criteria may not be interchangeable. For example, there is no direct numerical correlation between providing a view for an occupant and energy use.

6.5

Envelope Criteria

In order to design or redesign a building envelope, it is necessary to be clear about the components of that envelope and the tasks that each component is asked to perform. For most buildings, the two primary envelope components are the walls and the roofs, sometimes with secondary elements such as soffits and slabs on grade. Conceptually, there may be some crossover between these elements, such as a steeply sloping plane that performs some of the functions of roof and some of wall. For the sake of discussion, however, we will consider the parts of the envelope as they are most generally described.

Each component of the envelope must perform one or more tasks. These may include preventing or maximizing the flow of air between the exterior and interior, controlling conducted heat transfer, and protecting the interior from rain. The relationships between the envelope and the sun include controlling the quantity and quality of daylighting and solar heat gain. The envelope may provide access to views of the exterior from the interior. It may offer privacy to building occupants or may present views of interior activity to enliven the building's appearance. The envelope may encourage or discourage physical entry and may provide control and security. The envelope may be part of or independent from the building structure and will have inherent thermal mass properties.

Although the evaluation of sustainability is based on actual tasks performed, the envelope also communicates. It is the primary building element perceived by the public and, as such, conveys the building's meaning as an object in space, as an element in an urban fabric, as a component in the ecosystem, as a provider of needed services, as a place of civic pride or of spiritual elevation. The envelope may also educate, particularly about the interrelationships between the built and natural environments. This potential to inform and educate is immense.

Many of the above tasks are interconnected, sometimes in ways that support and reinforce each other. Sometimes a benefit in one area will be a cost in another. The architect must optimize the interplay among the multiple effects. In doing so, there will be aspects that are quantified in noncomparable units or, in some cases, not quantifiable. Judgment is needed.

The geometry of a building envelope will greatly impact its energy demands as well as its ability to meet program requirements. New buildings can be designed to optimize this geometry. Strategies for improving envelope performance of existing buildings must first consider the opportunities and limitations imposed by the given geometry.

6.6

Envelope Geometry

Building geometry—the size, proportions, and orientation of the envelope—will have a significant effect on design options for environmental performance of each major element of the envelope. The roof of a tall building will make up less of the overall envelope than will the roof of a single-story building; roof alterations or treatments will have less of an overall impact on a high-rise than on a low, spread-out structure. The shape and size of the envelope will establish the overall dimensions of the typical floor plate. The resulting distances of occupied spaces from the outside wall may limit the portions of the building that can be served by daylight and natural ventilation as well as what spaces can be given access to views. The relationship between these geometries and program accommodation will greatly affect the degree to which these assets are put to constructive use.

The aspect ratio of the plan—whether it is slender and long or nearly square—will inform the strategies to be considered for envelope design or modification. An elongated, narrow building will have two primary exposures and two secondary ones, whereas the four exposures of a square building

have roughly equal size. For the narrow building, it is critical to know whether the primary axis is generally north–south or east–west. For all building forms, the finer levels of orientation, whether the building is oriented on the cardinal compass points or biased to the east or west, will affect the relationship between solar impact and time of day.

Exposure to direct sunlight will argue for an envelope treatment for a south-facing perimeter zone that is different from one for a north-facing zone. Although the sun angles on a true east-facing wall will mirror those on a west-facing wall, the time of day that these occur, and therefore the relationships between solar impact and program, are likely to be totally different. While there may be geometric similarities between east and west zones, they are quite different in terms of building operation.

Some important generalizations can be made regarding primary orientations. For example, the most effective south-facing louvers or blinds will generally be horizontal, whereas those for east and west exposures will generally be vertical. It is rare, however, to be working with true north–south

orientation. The design of solar control must be based on the actual building orientation, not only for the geometry of the devices as they relate to solar angles but also to understand the relationship between solar impact and time of day as they relate to building use. Computer modeling tools allow hour-by-hour studies of the effects of alternate facade treatments on energy use and potential daylight harvest as well as of the expressive qualities of light and shade. Each facade may be optimized for its particular exposure.

Envelope design and performance are influenced by topology, the relationships among the parts. For example, as a rule it is easier to introduce solar control devices on the interior side of an envelope than on the exterior. On the inside, they are not subject to the effects of wind and rain. Maintenance, adjustment, and control are simpler, and the structural issues of attachment are less complex. On the other hand, interior devices will be less effective in controlling unwanted heat gain, particularly when used in conjunction with high-performance glazing.

Many of these principles can be seen in the South Jamaica Branch Library case study (see 9.3); however, they also represent conceptual foundations for solutions to a broad range of architectural problems. In the next chapter, specific building components and systems demonstrate the effect of these principles on the architectural design process.

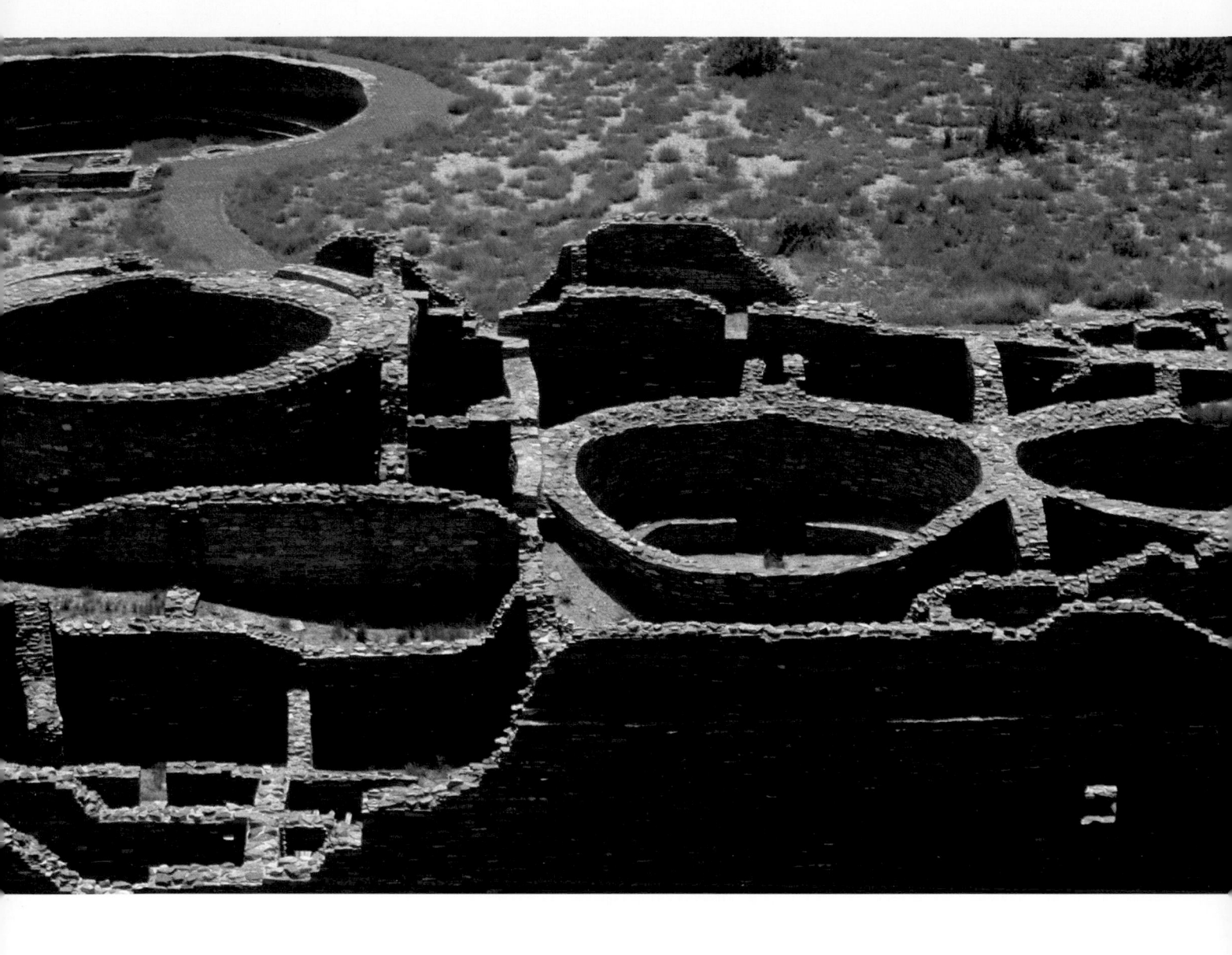

Chetro Ketl,
Chaco Canyon, New Mexico,
ca. 1100.

7

Process—Specific

Whether in new building design or existing building upgrade windows, glass, and glazing affect a wide range of issues, from quantifiable energy performance to considerations of thermal comfort, daylight benefits, and view. Newly developed, high-performance glazing products allow levels of design control that accommodate microconditions, including orientation of individual facades and specific programmatic demands. In synergistic strategies for overall building design or upgrade, the added costs for high-performance glazing will often be offset by savings in mechanical and electrical systems, resulting in comparable or lower overall first costs as well as significant operating savings.

7.1

Envelope and Glazing

Mica window, Acoma, New Mexico, ca. 1100.

The use of glass to allow light transmission through otherwise impervious walls dates to at least the Augustan period of Rome, 30–20 BCE. Each era of Western European architecture has been defined in large part by the ways in which glass was employed. Even cultures without glass technologies have sought the introduction of light through solid surfaces. Important architectural developments have evolved not only from advances in the use of glass itself but also from structural and construction innovations driven by the desire to create walls that can accommodate increased glazed areas.

Window glass is not a simple material. Historically, great efforts were applied both to coloring glass and to creating larger and more optically pure sheets. Contemporary glazing products may include multiple layers of glass and in some cases thin sheets of plastic; coatings and films to control light transmission, reflection, and emissivity; insulating gases in the cavities; and an edge assembly to join and seal the multiple layers. Performance varies widely. The insulating properties of some of the highest performing glazing products will be more than ten times better than that of single glass.

There is an almost unlimited range of shading coefficients, an ability to control unwanted solar gain.
However, there are trade-offs with each selection.
Higher insulation will inevitably result in at least
some loss of light transmission, affecting daylight
harvesting strategies. Glazing whose high shading
coefficient reduces summer cooling load will also
reduce direct solar heating gain in winter. At some
levels, shading will compromise views, the sense of
connection between indoors and out.

The selection of a particular glazing system will
be informed by many issues and by the interconnections among these issues. Glazing on the north
side of a building, where solar gain is not a concern,
can be optimized for daylighting and view, whereas
south-facing glazing in the same building may be
selected to limit unwanted heat buildup. If a room
has multiple exposures, a single-glazing system
may be selected to provide views that are consistent in brightness and color. The desired visual
connection to the outside will affect the selection of
shading coefficients. Glazing at a clerestory or roof
monitor that is out of the direct line of view can be
treated differently from that at eye-level windows.
All of these factors and many others will interact
to affect the availability of daylighting, energy
use for heating and cooling, and quality of space.
Energy performance can be effectively modeled
using the hour-by-hour simulations made possible
by such computer programs as DOE-2, which
was developed by the U.S. Department of Energy.
Modeling several extreme conditions for different

opposite

Transept, Notre-Dame de Chartres, Chartres, France, 1195–1260.

above

Rundetaarn (Tyco Brahe's Tower), Amsterdam, Holland, 1637–1642.

glazing products will establish baseline conditions. From these baselines, the combined effects of more subtle variations can be analyzed, creating trends in the changes in energy use patterns as glazing characteristics are adjusted on each exposure. The modeling can take into consideration the effects on heating, cooling, and lighting requirements. From these patterns, glazing can be optimized for overall energy performance. There are programs to model the daylighting efficacy of window designs. These will support a quantitative understanding, but will be of limited use for qualitative considerations.

While profoundly important from a sustainable perspective, quantified energy analyses do not take into account subjective effects, such as access to view and aesthetic considerations. It is at this point that architectural judgment comes into play. How does one weigh a 5 percent increase in cooling load against a visual connection to the outside world? And there are other more pragmatic but still unquantifiable factors to consider. For example, glazing with high insulating values and low emissivity will allow one to stand or sit by a large window on a cold day without feeling the discomfort of drafts or radiant heat loss inherent in traditional glazing. In this case, the negative factors will be the partial loss of light transmission, some effect on the appearance of the view through the window, and higher initial cost for the glazing product. The obvious benefits will be reduced cost of operating energy and greater comfort. A further systemic analysis of the interconnected conditions

Humble Administrator's Garden,
Suzhou, China, ca. 1500.

Great Hall, Shepard Hall,
City College of New York,
George Post, 1907.

opposite

High-performance glazing,
Croton-on-Hudson, New York,
Elemental Architecture,
2006.

above

Reflections (private house),
Carbondale, Colorado,
Tician Papachristou and Carl Stein,
1971 and 1993.

195 ENVELOPE AND GLAZING

and effects reveals other benefits. With conventional glazing, buildings in colder climates require heating at or near the windows in order to address both drafts and radiant heat loss due to the poor thermal performance. With high-performance glazing, heating at each window or glass area is no longer required, permitting a more compact, smaller mechanical system. The savings in the first costs of the mechanical systems will often be greater than the added costs of the optimized glazing. Through careful, smart design, operating cost savings and added comfort may be achieved with no added first cost.

Improved operating performance with equal or lower first costs represents not only an economic phenomenon but also a sustainable condition. The added resources required to manufacture the high-performance glazing may be fully offset by the reduced resources needed to produce the mechanical systems. In these cases, the break-even point occurs before the building is put into service. All operating savings are net, whether energy or economic. As with so much of sustainable design evolving from a Modern approach, this can be seen as doing more with less, an emphasis on smart, holistic strategizing and planning. But this is not a reduction in quality of life or compromise in human essentials. To the contrary, it can reconnect us to essential and deeply moving human experiences.

Replacement of conventional glass with high-performance glazing systems is one of the most effective measures that can be applied to an existing building envelope. The building components to be removed and replaced are generally discrete, independently supported, and of easily manageable size. Often, the original installation anticipated future replacement. Depending on the performance qualities of the glass being replaced, new glazing can reduce unwanted solar heat gain by four times or more and can cut conducted heat transfer—unwanted gains as well as losses—by as much as ten times. While this will somewhat reduce the amount of visible light admitted and the brightness of the view to the exterior, it will be far less with contemporary high-performance glazing than with the traditional darkly shaded glass, because new selective coatings are able to filter much of the unwanted solar radiation in the nonvisible ends of the spectrum.

One consideration in developing a reglazing strategy is whether the existing framing can dimensionally accommodate the new glass. Most older modern-style buildings have single glazing, typically varying from 1/8 to 1/4 inch in thickness. As a rule, the glazing stops on these frames cannot be adjusted to accept the thicker assemblies of contemporary high-performance systems, which will generally be 1 to 1 1/4 inches thick, which allows for two layers of glass and, sometimes, one or two sheets of transparent film within the air space.

If this is the case, a decision must be made as to whether it is more advantageous to replace the

existing framing or leave it and introduce a second glazing system inside or outside the original. If the existing glazing system is in good condition, adding new glazing inside the existing skin maintains the weather integrity of the building. For taller buildings, the new elements will not have to be designed to withstand the wind loading. This involves much simpler detailing and construction which, in turn, will result in lower cost. Problems with adding a second glazing layer include having more surfaces that require cleaning and access to operable windows. Depending on the reflectivity and emissivity of glazing used for the new interior layer, there may also be issues of excessive heat buildup within the new cavity. On the other hand, although more costly and generally more complicated, the replacement of the entire glazing system including the framing will allow the introduction of thermally broken frames as well as an opportunity to give the building a facelift.

Historic and architecturally significant buildings are a special case. Maintaining the original appearance of the glazing system will be of particular importance, sometimes to the exclusion of other considerations. Where window replacement is part of a renovation, close replicas of the original frames and sash can often be detailed to accommodate high-performance glass. If this is considered, it should be noted that the color and reflectivity of the new glazing will likely be noticeably different from the original. The level of the building's historic importance must be taken into account.

If maintaining the exterior appearance of the building is critical and environmental performance needs to be improved, a new interior sash may be appropriate. In this case, care must be exercised to minimize the reading of the new frame from the outside. Color and profile will be important. At the highest level of historic or architectural preservation, it

may not be appropriate to change the glazing system at all. Even with this restriction, comprehensive maintenance of hardware, weatherstripping, stops, and glazing compounds can significantly reduce unwanted air transfer

But as has been repeatedly noted, the purpose of architecture is not to save energy or other resources, but rather to use these valuable assets to meet needs, to satisfy program, a primary aspect of which is the satisfaction of human comfort. Improving the performance of a building's envelope will, in almost all cases, provide a more comfortable interior environment. While the upgrade of glazing systems will produce many benefits that can be quantified in both economic and sustainable measurement, the effort must ultimately address the extended and improved use of high-value resources as they serve the broader meaning of program.

The location of thermal mass within an envelope system, whether it is on the inner or outer surface and whether it is inside or outside the insulation, will alter how it affects the interior temperature. In existing buildings, it will affect the design of upgrades of mechanical and control systems.

7.2

Envelope and Thermal Mass

Contemporary envelope design generally incorporates insulation regardless of whether the construction has high or low thermal mass. This is unlike traditional high thermal mass buildings such as heavy masonry or adobe structures in which the envelope construction is essentially monolithic. The basic functioning of thermal mass was discussed in 4.7; however, the arrangement of the elements in a compound wall or roof system, in particular whether the thermal mass is inside or outside the insulation, will affect how the thermal mass functions. Its performance and its efficacy will be driven by a set of conditions, including outside and inside temperature cycles and building use patterns. The relationships among these factors and the interactions that result from these relationships are dynamic. The rates of change in temperature of each of the parts of the system, including the components of the envelope itself and the inside and outside air, will be different. Their cycles will be out of phase with each other, a characteristic instrumental to the flywheel effect, which tends to reduce temperature swings. Any analysis must cover a time period long enough to show the behavior of the complete system once it has reached a settled state.

above and overleaf
Sunlight is a primary source of energy supply to thermal mass storage, often heavy building materials, and simultaneously defines interior space and form. Rectory, Senanque Abbey, near Gordes, France, ca. 1150.

While the conditions of each project will be somewhat different, two examples suggest representative alternatives. In one case, consider a building that is in a cold climate but has high internal or direct solar heat gain. The building will have a tendency to overheat during the day. The heat resulting from the solar radiation or internal gain will cause the temperature of the air, which has a very low thermal mass, to rise above an acceptable level. If, however, a material with high thermal mass is placed somewhere inside the insulation, that same quantity of heat will be absorbed with a much lower

temperature rise than air, allowing that heat to be stored at an acceptably low temperature. At night, when there is no solar or internal heat gain, as the inside air temperature drops below that of the thermal mass material, the stored heat will be released, minimizing the need for additional heating. In this case, the thermal mass is providing energy storage.

In a second example, thermal mass placed outside of the building insulation may be used to mitigate the impact of exterior temperature extremes. During the day, when outside temperatures are above

above
St. Front, Perigueux, France, ca. 1100.

acceptable inside temperatures and the building is being cooled, a high thermal mass material on the exterior side of the building insulation will absorb heat with a lower temperature rise than would air. The result is that the exterior side of the insulation "sees" a temperature lower than the outside air temperature, and therefore the heat passing through the insulation into the building is less and cooling loads are reduced. At night, when outside temperatures drop below those in the thermal mass material, heat is released to the outside air, recharging the envelope system.

In addition to the options for the arrangement of thermal mass materials in a compound envelope system, performance can be optimized by its placement within the building volume. For example,

at the South Jamaica Branch Library, the heavily insulated sawtooth roof construction was kept thermally light to minimize the transfer of heat energy into the structure, thereby keeping more of this energy in the air where it is captured by the return air system and circulated throughout the building. The materials used near the floor level were selected for high thermal mass in order to store more heat energy at temperatures within the comfort range and to have this heat available in the occupied zones of the building. (See 9.3, "South Jamaica Branch Library.")

If the upgrade of an existing building includes recladding, the full range of options for the incorporation of thermal mass may be considered. If insulation is being added to an existing envelope, the placement of the insulation with respect to the existing mass will affect performance. It should be noted that, while outside the scope of this discussion, any changes in insulation must take into account the possibilities of creating conditions that cause internal condensation and, if appropriate, vapor barriers and drainage planes must be introduced. If the envelope is remaining generally unchanged, being aware of the existing thermal mass and understanding how it will affect the timing of temperature change will inform decisions regarding heating, cooling, ventilation, and control systems. Despite the inherent limitations imposed by the existing conditions, understanding issues of thermal mass will inform the upgrade of existing buildings, modern style or otherwise.

left
Notre-Dame de Chartres, tower stair,
Chartres, France,
1195–1260.

opposite
Kronborg Castle, tower stair,
Helsingor, Denmark,
ca. 1420.

The building envelope will control the passage of air between the exterior and interior. Using means such as operable windows or louvers, the envelope may be adjusted to encourage air transfer. Alternatively, the envelope itself may be fixed, with the building relying on mechanical systems to introduce outside air and exhaust inside air.

In building design or upgrade, the decision to provide ventilation using locally controlled, manual systems such as operable windows or automated mechanical systems will have as much to do with the emotional sense to be imparted by the space as by quantifiable environmental performance.

7.3

Envelope and Ventilation

One of the more controversial envelope conditions is direct, through-the-skin or "open window" ventilation. Its benefits include passive, nonmechanical operation, local direct control, and a sense of connection with the outside. Drawbacks include potentially problematic interactions with mechanical systems, lack of control of outside air quality and noise, and difficulties with automation and interconnection with building management systems.

Both the advantages and the disadvantages are real. As with many sustainable strategies, whether or not to use through-the-skin ventilation needs to be evaluated on a project-specific basis. Determining factors will include outdoor air quality issues, such as chemical and particulate pollution, pollen, and other allergens. It will include external noise levels and other distractions as well as security concerns. Most of all, however, the effective direct introduction of outdoor air will depend on climatological qualities, temperature, and humidity levels.

Despite the drawbacks, if the basic conditions justify its use, open window ventilation is not only a potential energy-saving measure but also one that can significantly enhance the quality of the interior environment. Connecting with nature has a strong positive emotional effect and offers valuable lessons about how we can carry out our lives synergistically with the natural environment. Operable windows also provide a level of local, individual climate control in which cause and effect are immediately apparent.

With modern technologies and controls, some of the drawbacks of operable windows can be mitigated. Relatively inexpensive sensors can monitor whether windows are open or closed. The output from these sensors can be used in a number of ways, from notifying building occupants or operators of the position of each window, to adjusting HVAC systems so that they do not work in opposition to or in duplication of the directly introduced outside air. Sensors may also control automated window operators and may be part of a building security program.

As noted in 6.3, when upgrading an existing building that was designed to take advantage of natural resources including open-window ventilation, understanding how it originally operated will often provide guidance for new or improved strategies.

Roofs, particularly in low-rise buildings, are often the most significant part of the interface between inside and out. Upgrading the performance of roofs and utilizing them for natural energy capture cannot be overlooked. At least as important are the opportunities inherent in overhead daylighting to enhance architectural experience, both in lighting and in spatial understanding.

7.4

The Roof

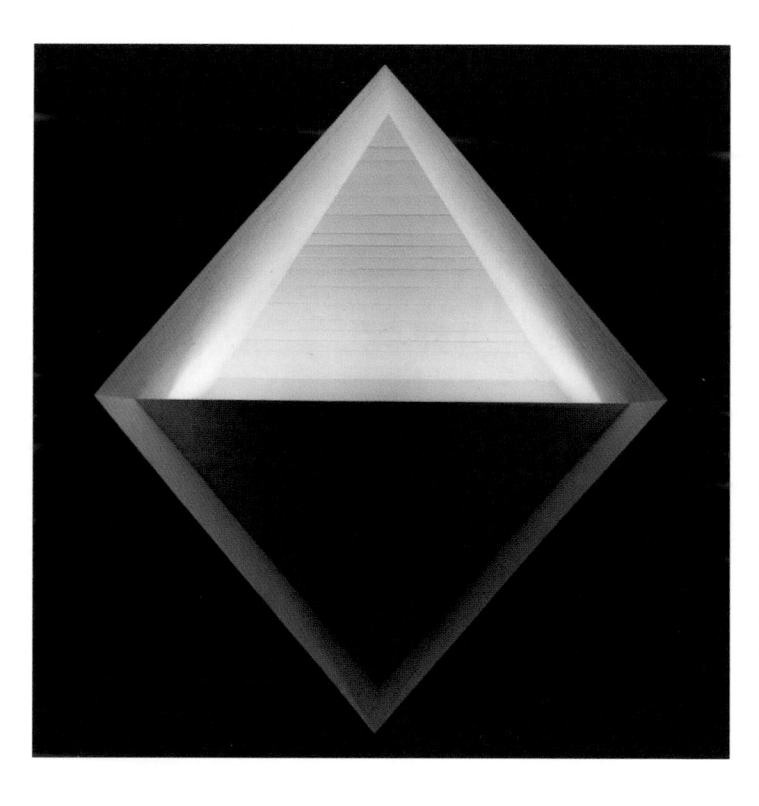

In addition to providing the light necessary for pragmatic functioning, skylights define architecture, creating drama, mood, static and dynamic sense of place, and mystery. St. Johns Abbey, Collegeville, Minnesota, Marcel Breuer and Associates, 1954–68 (MBA/GPS).

Roofs offer unique opportunities for environmental treatment; however, as noted earlier, the envelope geometry will dictate the potentials for benefits. The roof of a high-rise building will be small relative to the overall floor area as compared with a single-story structure. Roof measures may be at the heart of building-wide strategies for low buildings, but the same measures may become isolated gestures in taller structures and, further, may lose the advantages that come from the synergy of integration.

Generally, the most effective location for daylighting sources is overhead, from skylights, monitors, and clerestories. The light source, out of the primary field of view, creates less glare and unpleasant brightness. Overhead daylighting can be introduced anywhere on the floor, not limited to a zone near perimeter walls. The operation of dynamic shading devices is much less distracting when located overhead.

From a Second Law perspective, direct use of solar energy for daylighting will be significantly more effective than its conversion for electric lighting. The cost of installing a set of skylights is roughly

one-seventh the cost of a photovoltaic system that would produce an equivalent quantity of electric light. (See 8.6, "Skylights versus Photovoltaic Panels.")

Although the focus here is sustainability, not economics, the monetary cost is, at least to some degree, a reflection of any action's drain on society. It is certain that we will not have unlimited funds or resources to implement solutions to the energy and environmental crises. The degree to which we are successful in solving these problems will depend in large part on the cost and resource effectiveness of the measures applied.

An alternative roof surface will alter the effects a building has on its surroundings, perhaps controlling storm water discharge or the creation of heat islands, local hot spots caused by unusual solar heat absorption and storage. Roof treatment can also significantly change visual impact. In looking at options for roofing systems, it is essential to examine each alternative on the basis of clearly articulated goals. Before a particular green strategy is adopted, the reasons for its consideration must be cataloged and its efficacy in meeting those goals evaluated. For example, there is a tendency to think of planted roofs as been inherently environmentally beneficial. While there is no question that planted roofs address a number of environmental issues, many of these same issues can be met in other ways, sometimes more efficiently.

Planted roof systems offer insulating properties; however, the same levels of thermal resistance can be delivered by conventional insulation materials at a far lower cost. Conventional insulation weighs less than a planted roof, which reduces the amount of structure needed for the roof and for the columns

above and opposite
"Light scoops" above chapels at Notre-Dame du Haut, Ronchamp, France. Le Corbusier, 1954.

or walls supporting it. Planted roof systems greatly reduce the heat island effect caused by the absorption and release of solar energy. Roof systems with high reflectance and emissivity will have a similar effect, again at much lower cost and weight. Planted roofs will delay and reduce the release of storm water. Detention or retention systems using tanks or basins can do the same thing as can on-grade biofiltration. These measures significantly reduce or avoid the structural and waterproofing complications associated with green roofs.
A planted roof requires plant maintenance and possibly irrigation.

above
Cylindrical skylights in the chapel at the Convent of La Tourette, Eveux-sur-Arbresle, France. Le Corbusier, 1960.

opposite
Roof monitor, reflecting light shelf, and diffusing overhead baffle at the South Jamaica Branch Library, Queens, New York, TSP/Elemental Architecture, 1999.

On the other hand, where the roof is in view of surrounding land or buildings, a planted surface offers opportunities for greatly enhancing the vista. It will avoid the visual brightness of a reflective surface of a conventional high-performance roof and can incorporate decorative planting.

The form of the roof itself will affect options not only for daylighting but also for heat capture and gravity ventilation. At the South Jamaica Branch Library, traditional roof monitor forms coupled with active shading and lighting controls and stratified air heat recovery reduced energy consumption to less than half of other similar contemporary libraries. (See 9.3, "South Jamaica Branch Library.")

In new building design, the form of the roof can be an integral part of sustainable strategies. While there are generally limited opportunities to change the shape of the roof structure on an existing building, understanding the characteristics of the roofs on those buildings can inform the approaches to performance upgrade.

above
Planted roof, Maison Jaoul, Neuilly-sur-Seine, France. Le Corbusier, 1956.

opposite
The dining room in the new Headquarters for Rescue Company No. 1, New York City, includes the reinstallation of the first floor of the street façade from the original headquarters, destroyed in a 1985 fire. A linear skylight (upper left) accents the historic fragment, implies the continuation of the wall above the ceiling, and provides useful daylight. TSP/Elemental Architecture, 1988.

The essence of building control is to operate the building to achieve the best possible human conditions with the least negative environmental impact. Systems may be entirely manual or may be partially or totally automated.

7.5

Controls

Controls are the devices that cause building components or systems to operate in response to varying conditions or inputs. For sustainability, the control device must recognize what conditions are required to optimally meet program goals, what services must be delivered to achieve these conditions, and how these services can be delivered with the least environmental demand.

There are three basic parts of all control systems. The sensor measures the conditions that the building systems are intended to affect—temperature, light levels, air quality, and so forth. The processor evaluates the adequacy of the measured conditions, determines what adjustments would improve conditions, and then directs the operating mechanisms to make these adjustments. The operator carries out the instructions from the processor. Each part of the control system may be automated or manual.

There are several considerations to the selection of an automated or manual approach to controlling building operation. One is obviously cost. But even if cost is not a concern, there will be times when a manual system will be preferable. A totally automated control system can optimize building performance well beyond what could reasonably be expected from having the building occupants making real-time adjustments. While this leaves the users free to focus on other concerns, it essentially isolates them from information about how the building is providing the desired indoor environmental qualities. It creates a disconnect from a set of aspects basic to human life. If one of the programmatic goals of a building is to encourage an understanding of how individual decisions can affect sustainability, manual controls offer a direct means of communication, both in the immediately felt cause and effect relationships and, with proper interpretive elements, a grasp on the extended impact of individual action.

In many ways, a person may be the most elegant possible building control system. The entire system is totally integrated and self-adjusting. For example, consider the problem of direct sunlight creating glare on a computer screen and a window with a Venetian blind. The occupant senses that the level of sunlight entering the room is too great, the eye

is the sensor. The brain processes the information received by the retina, determines that an unacceptable condition exists, and that rotating the slats on the blind can eliminate the direct rays of the sun. It then directs the body to rotate the wand on the blinds. In a real-time operation, the sensor (eyes) observe the effect of the rotation on the entering sunlight, feeding the information to the processor (brain) which directs the operator (body) to stop at just the point that the direct sunlight is cut off.

While this example may seem overly simplistic, it is, in fact, not only seamless in its mechanisms and processes but also has the advantage of incorporating direct and immediate evaluations of the conditions to be controlled in terms of human reaction, rather than having to rely on a set of quantified criteria such as measurable light levels or contrasts, the values of which must then be correlated to appropriate conditions for human activity. This would appear to represent a perfect situation in that the performance conditions have been optimized to meet the user needs at the least possible environmental cost. Further, the immediately apparent cause and effect relationship is educational and potentially deeply satisfying.

At the same time, there are problems with a fully manual control option. It requires that a person be available to serve as the control system. Assuming that this is the user of the space, the responsibilities of controlling the interior environment may interfere with carrying out whatever else that person is

above and opposite
Direct solar gain atrium with large operable panels for ventilation. Note the relationship of building form and space with solar heating and convection cooling. Private residence, Shinnecock Hills, New York. TSP/Elemental Architecture, 1981.

doing. Additionally, there is nothing to insure that each user will control his or her portion of a building for optimal environmental performance. A frequently cited example of the drawbacks inherent in manual control is the person who in the winter turns the heat source too high and then opens a window when the room becomes too hot, this being the easiest set of actions to provide the desired temperature. We look at this and say, "How naive!"

Ironically, in the 1960s and '70s air-conditioning in many large buildings was controlled in essentially the same way. At a central mechanical plant, air was cooled to the lowest temperature that might be required anywhere in the building. To avoid overcooling the rooms, heating coils, generally electric, were provided to reheat the air to the desired temperature just before it was discharged. The heating coils were controlled by thermostats in each end-use zone so a high degree of local temperature control was achieved. The system was very simple and quite effective from the standpoint of control. The chillers and air delivery systems, being the more complex components, required little or no control. The components that provided the responsiveness were very inexpensive and very easy to control, requiring only an on-off switch responsive to the thermostat. The problem, obviously, was that this automated system took the inherent illogic of the blasting radiator and open window to a new level. Not only did the approach, called terminal reheat, rely on running an energy-consuming

system at full blast and then discarding the excess work done (in this case, cooling), it used a second energy-consuming system to overcome the excess. And while some terminal reheat systems did use steam or hot-water coils, many used electric heating coils because of their low first cost and simple control. The inherent inefficiency of electric resistance heating, a Second Law phenomenon, was yet another source of energy waste. It was as though the person who had been opening a window to mitigate the overheating decided instead to turn on an air conditioner.

Controls may be simple or complex. A thermostat controlling a heating system is a complete, simple control system. It measures the ambient temperature, compares it to a preset reference point and, if the measured temperature is below the setpoint, activates a switch that causes the heating system to operate. It is the sensor, the processor, and the operator. A timer controlling a light fixture is also a simple control in which the sensor is the clock, the processor is the pins that designate whether the light is on or off at a particular time, and the operator is a switch activated by the movement of the pins. Combining these two devices produces a slightly more complex control device, the clock thermostat, which allows different setpoints for different times of day.

In each of these examples, the users of the controls have established one or more "if criterion X, then action Y" scenarios. The design criteria and result-

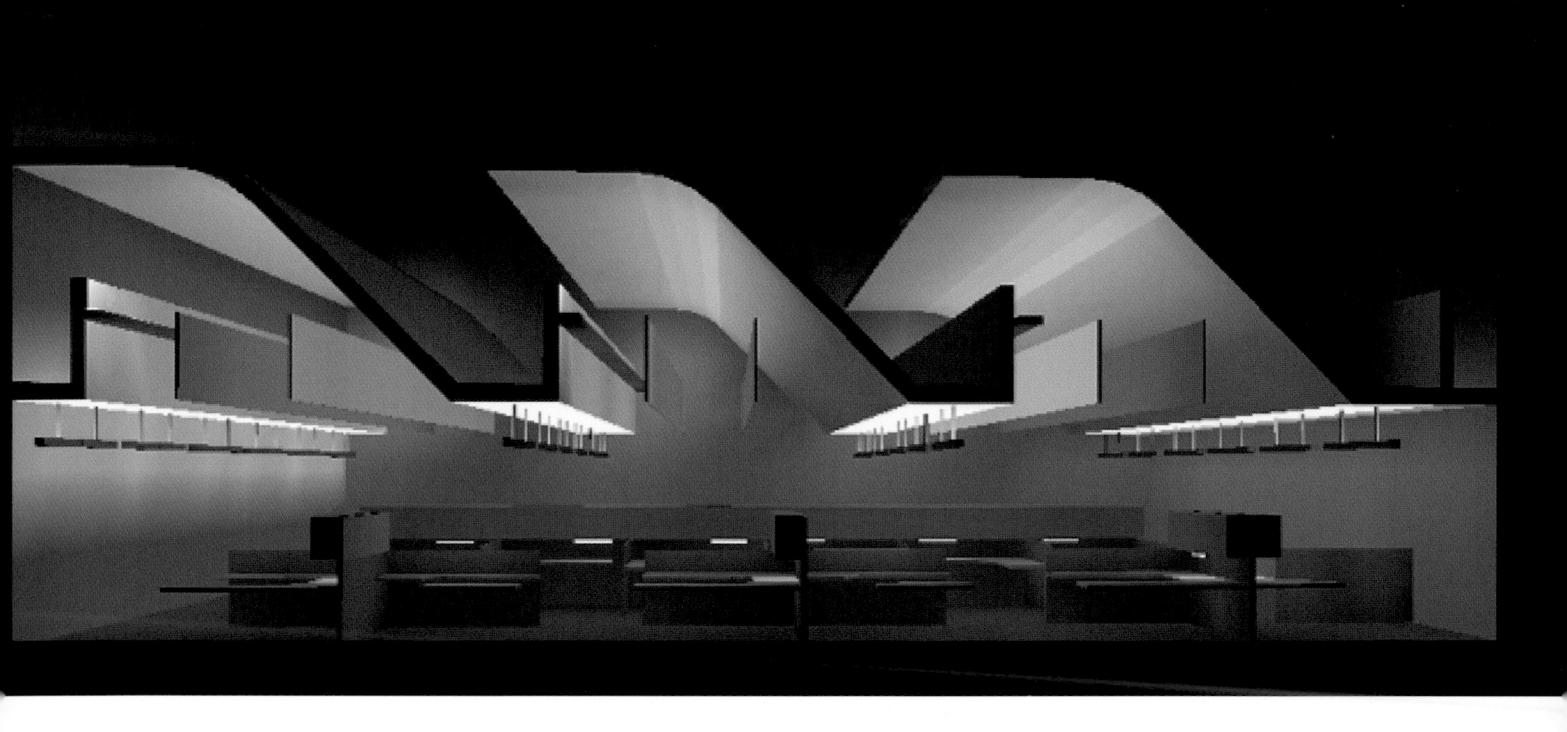

opposite

The saw-tooth roof at the South Jamaica Branch Library, Queens, New York, accommodates south-facing monitors with active shading devices and reflecting/diffusing panels delivering even light to the reading room. The shape also creates natural collection points for hot air that is recirculated in the winter and exhausted in the summer (see 9.3). TSP/Elemental Architecture, 1999.

above

Computer-generated lighting study for new NYS DEC regional office building which employs daylighting and heat-recovery strategies similar to the South Jamaica Branch Library. Brandston Partnership, Inc., lighting designers, 2003.

ing actions approximate those of a human operator monitoring building conditions and operating one or more pieces of equipment.

The advent of digital controls dramatically expanded the number of criteria that could be reasonably monitored and greatly increased the refinement of the control offered by simple systems. There are, however, several unavoidable drawbacks to this added complexity. Building operation has become less apparent. Correlations between cause and effect are masked with the result that building users have become increasingly unaware of the impact their actions have on system operation. Further, the users have less sense of the changing exterior conditions. For the most part, this disconnect compromises the quality of the built space. Yet controls can transcend these limitations when the criteria for their operation considers the program imperative to touch the heart and elevate the spirit, particularly in areas that connect us to the natural environment and inform us as to the interrelationships of our actions.

Controls for the South Jamaica Branch Library in Queens, New York, were developed to engage the building users while maximizing environmental performance. They were also designed to limit the need for library staff attention, which was anticipated to be focused primarily on library issues. The building makes extensive use of controlled daylighting, direct solar gain, and capture and recirculation of stratified solar-heated air during the winter, and

exhaust of that stratified air during the summer. Daylighting, primarily from overhead monitors, is provided with active shading. The control system consists of two basic parts, the lighting and shading controls and the HVAC controls. The operations of these two parts are interconnected.

The lighting/shading control system limits the daylight levels whenever excessive light levels would add a load on the building's cooling system, and maximizes daylight levels when the associated heat gain would reduce the load on the heating system. This is triggered by the HVAC system signaling to the lighting control system whether it is operating in a heating or cooling mode. This is the only connection required between lighting and HVAC systems.

Any light in the building, whether from daylight or electric fixtures, will eventually become heat. In the winter, the maximized daylight levels heat the air, which rises to the high points at the roof monitors where it is collected and recirculated, heating the thermal mass of the entire building. In the summer, the heat that results from maintaining the minimum light levels is significantly reduced from that captured during the winter, but heat is unavoidable. The heated air rises to the roof peaks but now is exhausted, rather than recirculated, thus reducing the load on the air-conditioning system. The effect of the lighting control system on the HVAC controls comes from the increased or decreased heat in the building which, in turn, is "seen" by the HVAC controls through the temperature sensors.

Each component of the control system is conventional and relatively simple; however, they function as a highly effective integrated whole when combined with a building form that optimizes the potential for solar and thermal control and when programmed to take advantage of the complex interactions among the conditions that exhibit diurnal and seasonal cycles. (See 9.3, "South Jamaica Branch Library.")

The heat recovery and exhaust approach at the South Jamaica Branch Library was based on a much simpler, early direct solar gain residential project (see pages 218–219). Program issues unrelated to environmental performance suggested a vertical arrangement of interconnected spaces. This produced a design in which heated air naturally is collected at the top of the building. The supplemental heating system forced hot air. A return duct was added connecting the high point of the house to the furnace. The control system consists entirely of two conventional thermostats. The first, located at the peak of the house, operates the furnace fan. Whenever the collected hot air reaches a temperature of at least 78 degrees, the fan draws hot air to the furnace and distributes it throughout the house. A second thermostat, located in the living and dining area, set at 68 degrees, has a conventional connection to the furnace. When the redistributed air is not adequate to heat the space, the furnace burner fires and makes up the difference. The only items that had to be added to create what proved to be a highly effective heat recovery system were one simple thermostat and about twenty feet of 12-inch round duct. The control system was based on identifying two very easily measured conditions that could trigger two simple modes of operation, already intrinsic to the heating system.

The same basic approach was used for the design of a new office building for the New York State Department of Environmental Conservation. An new underfloor air distribution system increased the effectiveness of thermal storage and added flexibility for future planning changes. The site configuration also permitted the use of windows with light shelves, coupled with active shading.

The lighting control strategy employed at the library in Queens is extremely effective in reducing the energy demands for lighting, heating, and cooling. Equally, or perhaps more important, are the spatial enhancements that result from the connection with the natural environment. A year and a half after the South Jamaica Branch Library opened, one of the managers commented that she found that in the summer, when the light levels were limited, coming in from the outside was like walking into a grove of shade trees while in the winter, the brighter interior space created a noticeable sense of warmth and comfort. Although we did not specifically plan for these effects, the result was inherent to the process in which the power of nature was a primary driver of the fundamental architectural design.

8

Observations

Geometry is the grammar of architecture. It gives order to the architectural design process, provides the tools that allow control of the act of architecture, and helps to explain the experience of architecture.

8.1

Geometry and Understanding

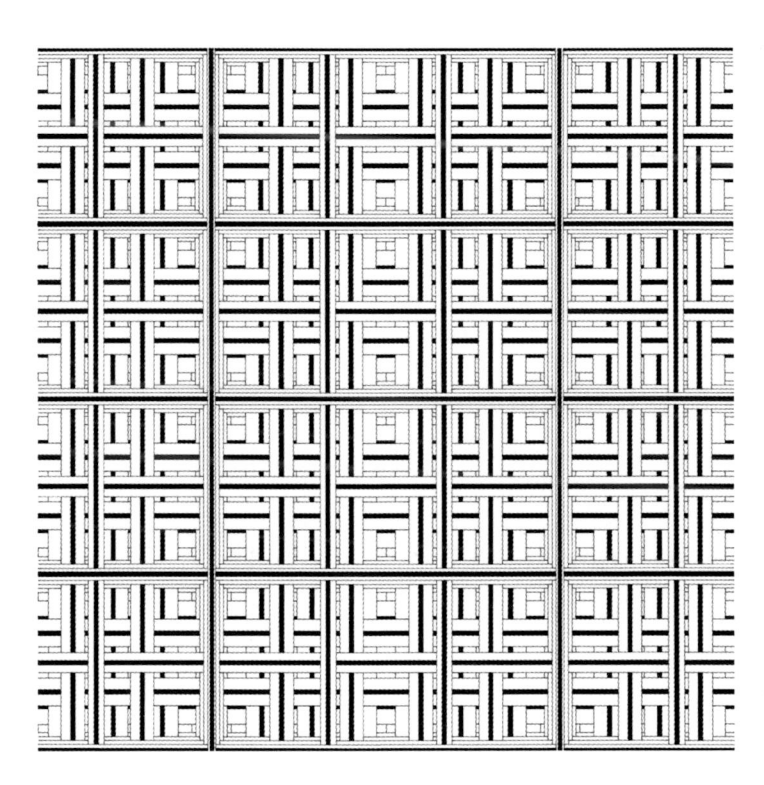

Line Field
(After Red Shift), ink on paper,
Dan Kleeman, 2007.

Architecture facilitates. It allows us to understand the interplay between the activities of our lives and the physical context within which we operate. This context is broad. It includes geometric issues in two and three dimensions. Planar geometry addresses concerns that range in scale from the plans and elevations of individual, personal spaces to the organization of sites, cities, regions, and nations. It makes comprehensible our place within systems that can be expressed as surface.

It may be argued that we don't live in a planar world, that we are creatures of volume and space. This is true, but it does not negate the underlying fact that many of our activities are best represented in two-dimensional terms. For example, a very large percentage of our travel occurs within a space whose vertical axis relative to the horizontal axes is so small that it may be ignored, thus the value of traditional maps.

Similarly, building plans allow us to comprehend and control the interactions of programmatic function and space to the extent that are generated by ground and floor organization. As with any repre-

sentation, what is shown is limited and must not be confused with the holistic totality, only a portion of which is being displayed.

Three-dimensional or spatial geometry addresses issues of building form, volume, and space, and of grade and terrain. It also allows consideration of movement in space, this last aspect covering both the vertical offset of what are otherwise planar systems, such as with overpasses and tunnels, and true vertical movement systems, including stairs, escalators, and elevators. Their incorporation into planning and building design is the basis for the stacking necessary to produce the densities that result in the efficiencies of resource utilization inherent in contemporary urban conditions. It also supports the conceptual possibility of simultaneous occupancy of position, at least to the extent that location is defined on a two-dimensional projection, generally plan location.

The understanding of spatial positioning is both intellectual and intuitive. It is analytic and pragmatic, but it is also emotional and spiritual. It may be presented directly and clearly, but it may also be intentionally subtle and ambiguous. To experience architecture is to experience geometry. Architecture can also speak of other relationships between the individual and the greater physical world. In many if not most cases, the vehicle is the envelope which is quite literally the interface between the interior spaces that the building creates and the context—natural and built. The use of architectural

above and opposite

Façade of Headquarters for Rescue Company No.1 organized by three overlapping grids, New York. TSP/Elemental Architecture, 1988.

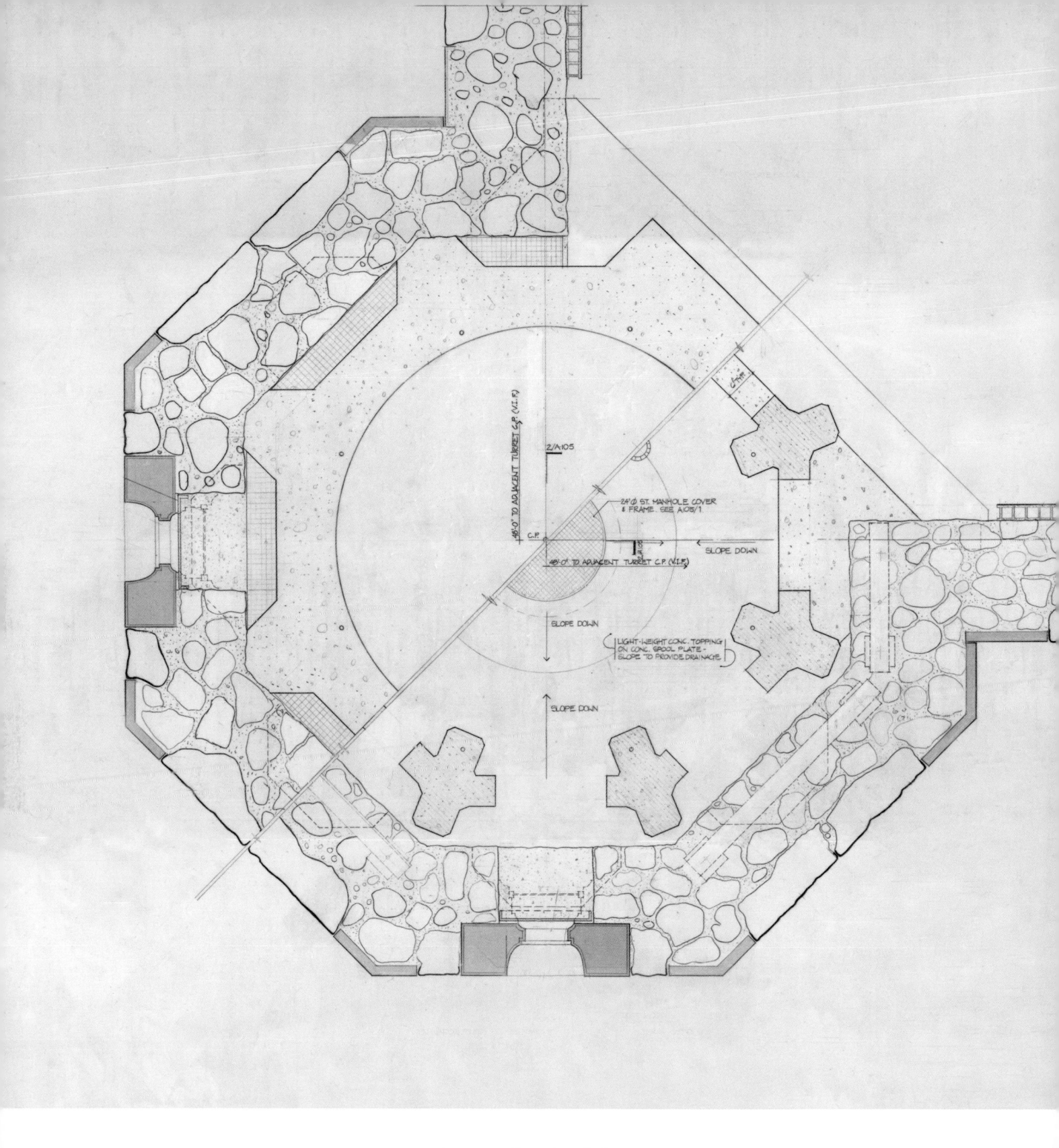

2/A105

24"⌀ ST. MANHOLE COVER
& FRAME. SEE A105/1

SLOPE DOWN

C.P.

46'-0" TO ADJACENT TURRET C.P. (V.I.F.)

48'-0" TO ADJACENT TURRET C.P. (V.I.F.)

SLOPE DOWN

SLOPE DOWN

LIGHT-WEIGHT CONC. TOPPING
ON CONC. SPOOL PLATE.
SLOPE TO PROVIDE DRAINAGE.

above, opposite, and overleaf
"CAT scan" analysis of turret at the Main Tower of
Shepard Hall, CCNY showing relationships between
new structural core and new cladding at 17 different
elevations. TSP/Elemental Architecture, 1987.

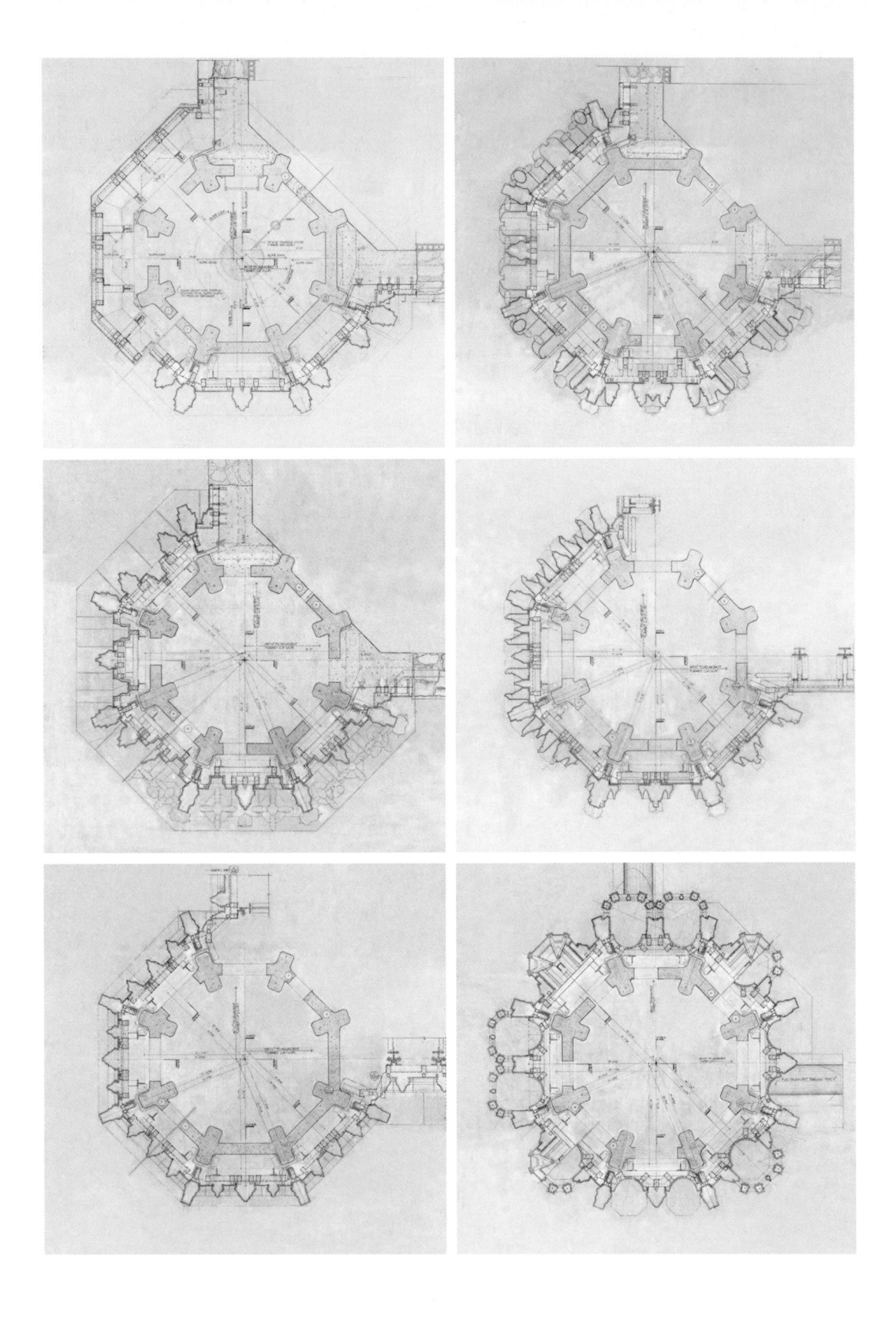

elements to control, exploit, and display sunlight connects the viewer to the dynamic conditions of climate, season, and time of day. This may be seen in the changing sizes and angles of shadows, the transformation of the appearance of glass from transparent to reflective or opaque as light conditions shift, the waving of a banner in response to changing breezes. The analytical design tool that supports the understanding and control of these phenomena is geometry. While this may be seen simply as an application or manipulation of the effects of a particular form of renewable energy, it is also an intuitively felt demonstration of profound and inescapable forces that impact all humankind. This appreciation of the world and its cycles connects us to concepts and conditions that transcend our existence as individuals in both space and time. The understanding of sustainability that results from this appreciation goes far beyond the substitution of one resource or technology for another. It fundamentally changes what we value, what we consider to be the essence of quality of life.

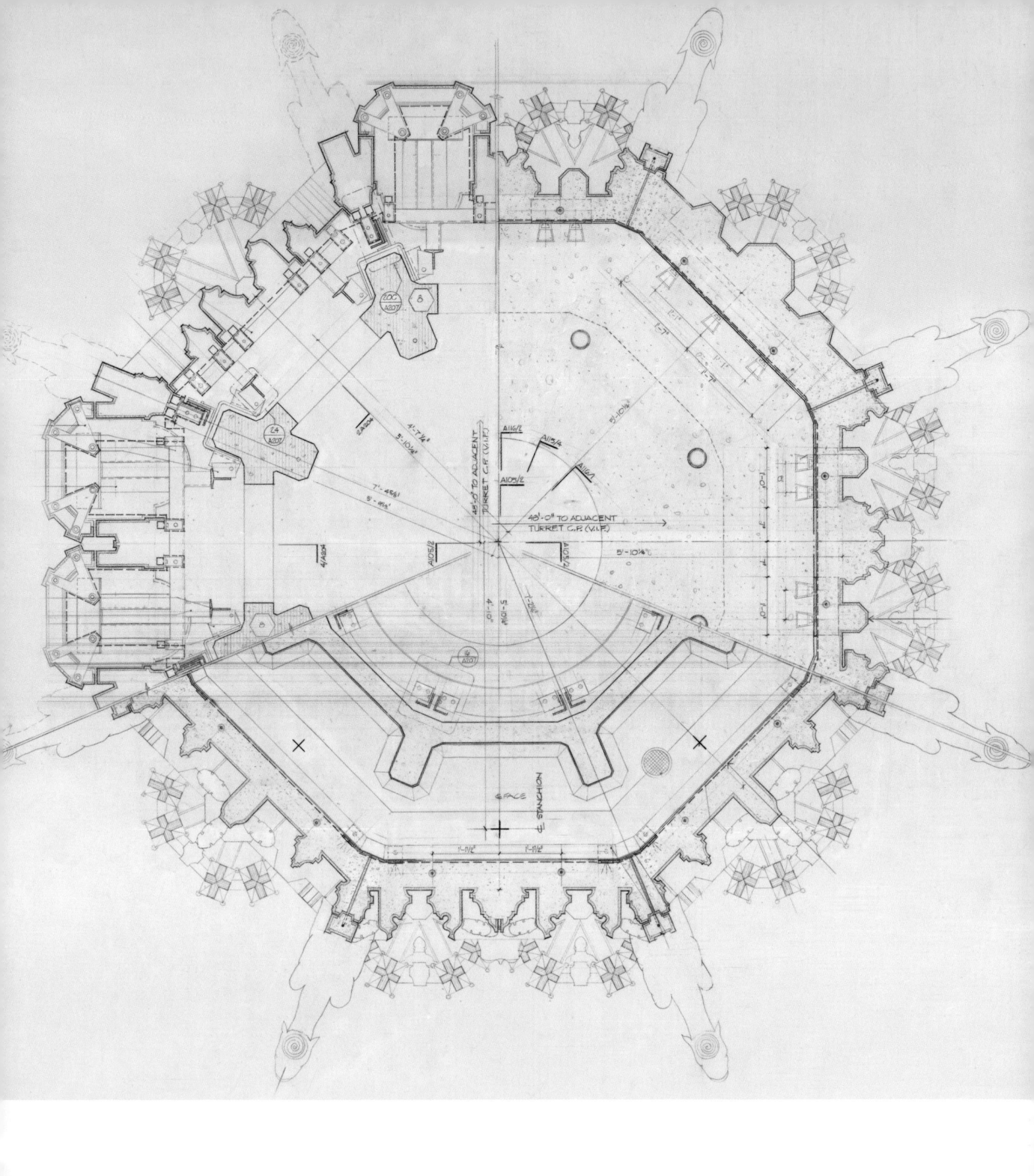

A work of architecture can, in itself, provide or lead to many levels of understanding. When this results from the fundamental design approach, the benefits are achieved with no added commitment of resources.

8.2

Architecture and Understanding

Decisions regarding building design, including form and materials, entrance, orientation, and scale, among many others, can speak eloquently of such complex issues as the relationships between humankind and the rest of the ecosystem, between the built and the natural environments, between contemporary culture and cultural history, between the individual and society, between immediacy and historic continuity. Nowhere is this more apparent than in the use of apertures to direct the visual experience of context—whether natural or built. To the extent that these understandings derive from the underlying bases of the architecture, they are achieved at no added resource cost.

Moreover, when communication of fundamental aspects of our condition in space and time results from experiencing the essential activities and objects of our existence, the resulting understanding is inherently authentic, as opposed to learning based on simulations or overlays. Architecture offering such communication is supported by, if not an inevitable result of, the conceptual clarity that is integral to both Modern process and Modern design. This applies to both simple and highly complex works, as long as the simplicity or complexity is appropriate to a particular project.

Apertures, both found and constructed, control views and provide understanding of object, of context, of relationships between viewer and vista while simultaneously allowing passage of light, air and objects.

above left
Opening in ancient pathway, Canyon de Chelly, Arizona.

above right
Entry to "Balcony House," Mesa Verde, Colorado.

opposite left
Pueblo Bonito, Chaco Canyon, New Mexico.

opposite right
Dorsoduro, Venice, Italy.

Archways, while providing physical passage, frame and direct views to inform and enrich the entry experience.

top left

Entry to Piazza San Marco, Venice, Italy.

top right

Silvacane Monastery. La Roque-d'Anthéron, France, ca. 1200.

above

Verona, Italy.

opposite

Openings in the site wall surrounding fragments of the 1843 Wesleyan Chapel present historic artifacts and juxtapose them against evidence of longstanding neglect. Unfortunately, in 2009–10 the Park opted to replace the evocative monument with an approximated replica of the original building. Women's Rights National Historical Park, Seneca Falls, New York. TSP/ Elemental Architecture with Ann Marshall and Ray Kinoshita, 1993.

A conceptual basis of Cubism is the creation of a synergistic whole resulting from simultaneous interactions among multiple, sometimes seemingly contradictory, factors. This provides insight for the development of holistic planning and architectural designs that include sustainability as a primary criterion.

8.3

Cubism, Sculpture, and Architecture

The evolution of Modern thought closely paralleled the development of Cubism. These movements influenced each other and were informed by the same set of cultural, social, and scientific events; in particular, the clarification of complex questions by the detailed articulation of the issues and the analysis of the alternatives. The transformative power of Cubist painting draws heavily on the control of time to allow the superposition of two objects or simultaneous views of the same object to occur within a flat plane. Prior to the understanding of time as a dimension, this superposition was conceptually impossible in a two-dimensional composition. Cubist paintings treat singular conditions viewed simultaneously from multiple positions. The painter's skill and sensibilities determine how this information was presented.

The Cubists' insistence on the flatness of the canvas is underlined by the incorporation of unmistakably planar elements such as partial newspaper pages. As such this differs from work based on multiple images, as with the Futurist "Nude Descending a Staircase" by Duchamp, where the subject rather than the viewpoint has moved, and the resulting work is essentially multiple conventional perspectives.

When a work becomes three-dimensional, as with sculpture or architecture, the tension and meaning resulting from the simultaneity of viewpoints vanishes. One can actually walk around a piece of sculpture, seeing it from all sides and employing real time rather than time as a concept. The experience of a building involves both time and movement. That certain midcentury buildings incorporate Cubist forms is the result of an appreciation of those forms, rather than an application of Cubist theory.

While the forms of Cubism applied to architecture do not, in themselves, carry the substance of Cubist thought to a building, Modernist thought informed by early Cubist work regarding the experience of form and space is highly relevant to making buildings more sustainable. In particular, the dense overlays of form and meaning inherent in Cubist paintings reference the fact that any building

element or any space within a building may be acting in a number of different ways at the same time, and that each of these activities are part of highly complex, integral whole.

For example, a window may admit light, allow view, be operable to introduce outside air, affect heat transfer, and by its shape and detail, speak to the use of the building. These multiple functions of a single building element will interact with the heating, cooling, ventilation, and lighting systems and building thermal mass. They will relate to the vertical and horizontal dimensions of the room, the furniture layout, and the reflectivity of interior finishes. Windows will affect how the exterior world is seen from the interior and, simutaneously, how the building is perceived from the outside.

It is the multilayered meaning and function of each element of building design, rather than a formal overlay of style, that connects a Modern approach with Cubism. This applies to all aspects of the design process; however, it is particularly helpful regarding the understanding of building form as related to sustainable performance. Consideration of where functions are located within a building, the efficiency of space use, access to daylight, useful direct solar heat gain, the view as a workspace enhancement, adjacency to other functions, and interior circulation and way-finding will each affect sustainability to a greater or lesser degree; the impact from the interrelationships among these factors and the synergies that result will be far more significant.

Modernism provides both the vision to address complex problems in their complexities and the tools, or at least the proto-tools, to bring clarity and order to the multilayered sets of information without having to resort to oversimplification.

Carpenter Center, Cambridge, Massachusetts.
Le Corbusier, 1964 (Ezra Stoller © ESTO).

Le Corbusier's Carpenter Center at Harvard is one of the few buildings that utilizes the concepts of Cubism to achieve architectural ends. The ramp detaches and lifts the "ground plane" above the actual ground, allowing the building to be entered at its midpoint, horizontally and vertically. The programmatic, circulatory, and formal organization are all highly center-weighted with all internal movement going from the core to the perimeter.

8.4

Topology of the Carpenter Center

The Carpenter Center is often described as an architectural manifestation of Cubism. This view is generally based on the appearance of the building and, as such, is incorrect on two counts. An integral part of Cubist concept is the interplay between the dimensions of space and time and the implied use of time to overcome spatial impossibilities. A three-dimensional formal work viewed in a three-dimensional context, whether architecture or sculpture, will not involve as a generating idea the contradiction of the spatial superposition of objects resolved through the manipulation of time. Further, Le Corbusier's own painting and sculpture, which presage the form of the Carpenter Center, were explicitly non-Cubist. He described these works, which represent objects in strongly geometric semi-abstractions, as "Purist." Ambiguity between the two-dimensional reality of the canvas and the need for a third dimension to accommodate subject material is not addressed. The forms of Carpenter Center are definitely Purist rather than Cubist.

Yet the spatial and volumetric organization of Carpenter Center, its topology, owes much to Cubism.

This is a building whose main entry is at the center of the volume, horizontally and vertically. There are many buildings, either executed or proposed, in which one is brought into the core of the space, such as Buckminster Fuller's geodesic structure for the US pavilion at Expo '67 in Montreal or Étienne-Louis Boullée's spherical cenotaph for Sir Isaac Newton. However, in each of these examples, the experience of entry is masked, as if the architects would have preferred to have transported visitors into their buildings with the wave of a wand.

In the case of the Carpenter Center, the means of getting to the core of the volume—the iconic ramp—is not only a profoundly important element in the composition, it clearly insists that the entry route remains part of the exterior until it reaches that core. The ramp is at once part of the sidewalk and part of the building, ground and figure. In the same way that a Cubist painting presents simultaneous views of the subject within a single, flat plane, the ramp presents a "ground" condition that is three stories above the actual ground plane. While this is conceptually fascinating, it also gives

usage and experiential options that are not possible with traditional ideas of ground conditions and entry points.

Reuse of existing buildings must include, at the very least, consideration of the options for reorganizing activities with respect to the building form, essentially restructuring the topology. In some cases, an actual transformation of the topology may be appropriate, either through modification of the structure or of the circulation systems,

U.S. pavilion, Expo 67, Montreal. Buckminster Fuller, 1967 (R. G. Stein).

View toward the sidewalk from the main public entry at the third floor of the Carpenter Center, Cambridge, Massachusetts. Le Corbusier, 1964.

The Congrès Internationaux d'Architecture Moderne (CIAM) formulated a matrix to display the interrelationships of the diverse considerations that informed and affected urban planning and architecture. The approach suggests a basis for evaluating and executing sustainable design.

8.5

CIAM Grid

The history of Modernist efforts to structure the process of planning and design offers a framework for establishing the criteria and quantifying the impacts of sustainable design alternatives. Beginning in 1928, the CIAM sought to establish a basis for identifying and organizing the problems that needed to be addressed by planning and architecture and to display the solutions subsequently developed. For nearly thirty years, many noted architects, planners, and theoreticians including such diverse practitioners as Alvar Aalto, Hendrik Berlage, Victor Bourgeois, Le Corbusier, Lucio Costa, Cornelius Van Eesteren, Sigfried Giedion, Walter Gropius, Walter Loos, Richard Neutra, Gerrit Rietveld, Josep-Lluís Sert, and Mart Stam met to identify the primary issues to be addressed by Modernism and to propose solutions to those issues.

Beginning with the broadest terms, CIAM defined the problems to be solved by urbanism as those of dwelling, working, and recreation, and the elements to be manipulated to optimize these conditions as the ground plan, circulation, and public policy. From this apparently simple basis, successively finer detail was introduced that incorporated a dense layering of information and accommodated considerations as apparently subjective as aesthetics and ethics. In 1947, two decades of investigation were summarized and presented in the CIAM grid, a graphic matrix intended to facilitate urban and architectural design and to communicate the issues to persons and organizations outside the design professions. The vertical axis redefined the problems of Modern architecture as Living, Working, Care of the Body and the Spirit, and Circulation. The horizontal axis contained double headings, the first set being the themes or general avenues for responding to the problems and the second being suggestions as to what the specific reactions might be. Within the grid, at the intersection of a problem, a theme and a reaction to the theme, the cell, which represented the proposed solution, was often an image rather than a verbal statement. In other words, the grid provided an armature for sketching solutions to individual parts of a complex problem without losing sight of the whole.

Many of the solutions suggested by the CIAM grid seem naive by current standards. One reason is the inevitable comparison between the power inherent

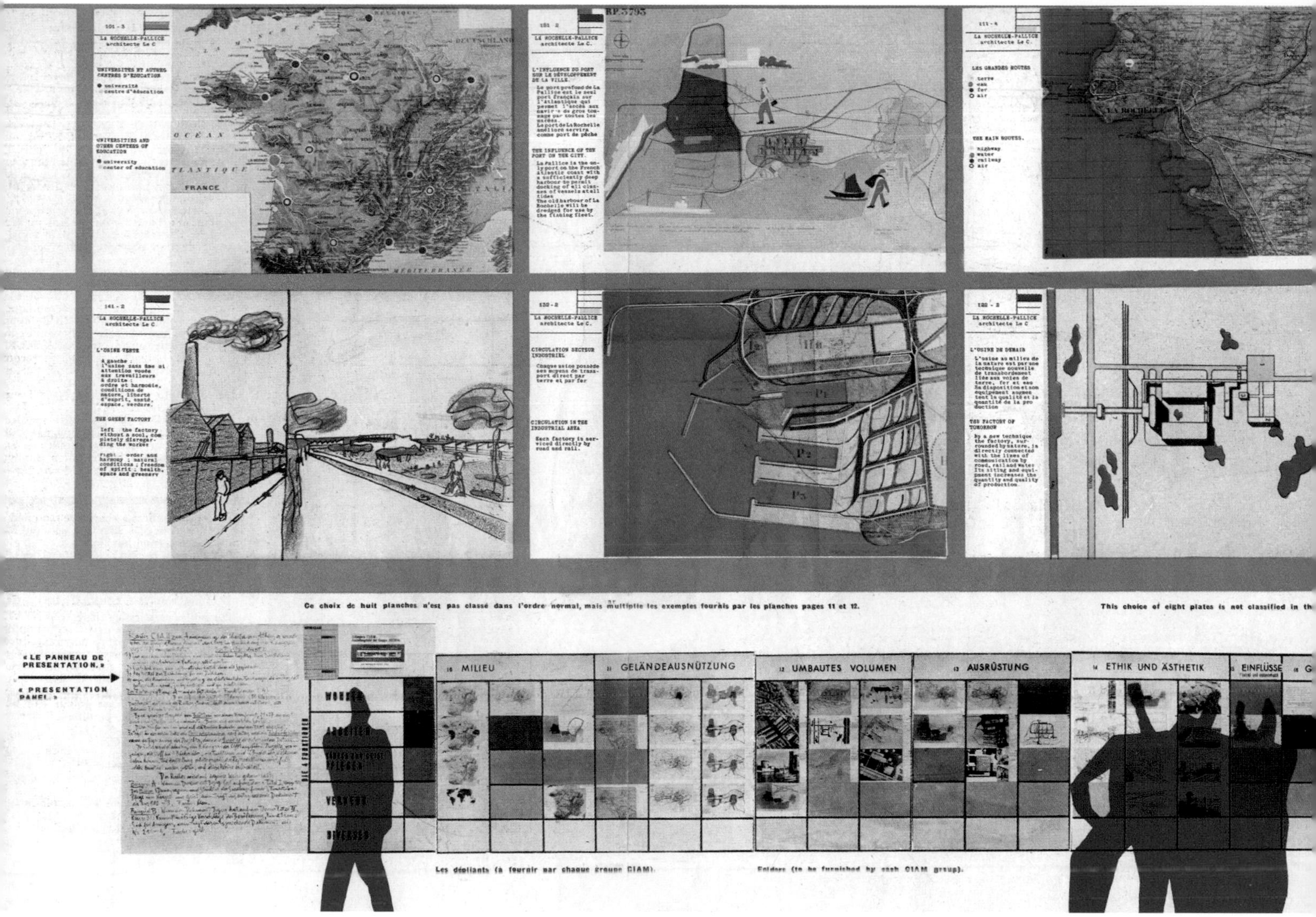

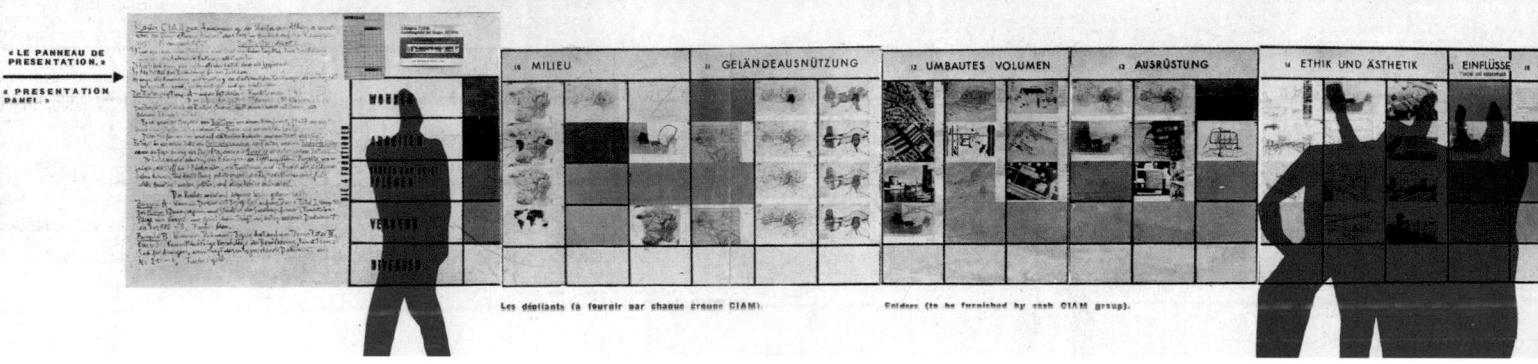

in digital tools for information management and limitations imposed by the handmade grid. Yet the nonverbal solutions put forward in the sketches and diagrams suggest a subtlety that is difficult to match with words and numbers. Another issue with the CIAM grid, and in fact with most Modern planning, design, and theory, is that issues at the forefront of current concerns, in particular that resources are finite, were simply not within the field of view of the Modern architects of the 1920s, '30s or '40s. However, neither the improvements in data management technologies nor the understanding of the added problems imposed by finite resources negates the importance of the Modern tenets that correlate basic human needs with the resources committed to their achievement.

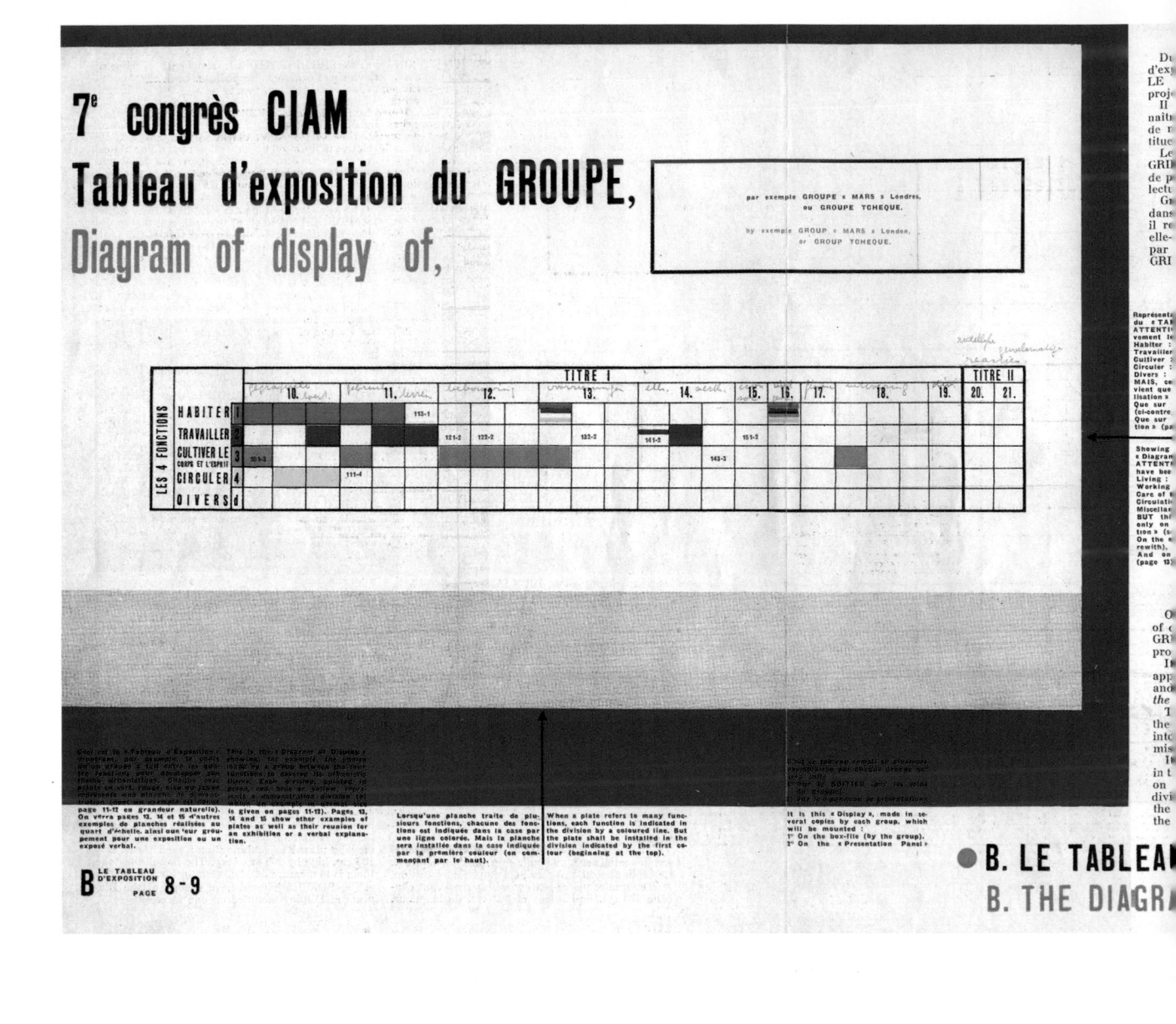

opposite and above
Details of the CIAM grid.

A comparison between the direct introduction of daylight and the conversion of daylight into electricity used to power electric light fixtures demonstrates the environmental as well as economic costs of complexity.

8.6

Skylights versus Photovoltaic Panels

Consider a typical 750-square-foot school classroom that depends on electric lighting for two thirds of its area, 500 square feet. The lighting load for this, assuming a relatively efficient design, might be 750 Watts. If the inclusion of skylights for daylighting caused the lights to be turned off 1,000 hours per year, the energy saving would be 750 kilowatt-hours. This energy saving comes at what is generally peak demand time and represents operating cost savings of anywhere from $45 to more than $150 per year. It also represents the saving of about 60 gallons of oil or its equivalent at the generator. Applied to a school for 1,000 students, that is, forty classrooms, this one measure would each year save 30,000 kilowatt hours at the building or the equivalent of 2,400 gallons of oil at the generator, representing savings of up to $6,000 per year.

Is the measure worth the cost and effort? Assume that each classroom receives two small skylights or light tubes, which cost $300 when installed in a new building or during a renovation involving a roof replacement. The cost is $600 per classroom, or $24,000 for the school. While this may seem high, consider the cost of a wind turbine that would generate 30,000 kilowatt-hours per year. Current estimates are that wind generation costs between $1,500 and $2,400 per installed kilowatt in wind farms and around $3,000 for small installations. With a utilization rate of 25 percent to account for wind speed variation, one installed kilowatt will generate 2,190 kilowatt-hours per year. Generating 30,000 kilowatt-hours per year would require about 13.7 installed kilowatts. At $2,000 per kilowatt, this would cost about $27,400, exclusive of storage.

While individual costs may vary, the overall costs for equivalent skylight and basic wind turbine systems are roughly the same, however, these alternatives are not directly comparable. The wind turbine is considered to operate day and night, year-round, 8,760 hours, while the skylight is considered to be productive for only 1,000 hours per year. The wind turbine must therefore either be connected to a utility grid that can constructively use the output whenever the classrooms are not in use, or be equipped with storage capacity for the energy collected during periods when the classrooms are not in use. Without storage, if its output were only captured and used when needed by the classrooms,

the capacity would have to increase by almost nine times, making the cost of the wind system about ten times that of the skylights. If the wind turbine system is connected to the utility grid, much of its output will be delivered during nonpeak times when the economic and environmental values are lower. If storage is used, the economic and environmental costs of constructing that system must be taken into account.

Looking at a photoelectric alternative, current estimates are that photovoltaic (PV) generation costs $10,000 per installed kilowatt. With a utilization rate of 20 percent to account for nighttime hours and cloud cover, one installed kilowatt will generate 1,752 kilowatt-hours per year. Generating 30,000 kilowatt-hours per year would require about 17 installed kilowatts. At $10,000 per kilowatt, this would cost $170,000. The times when solar energy is available to the PV system will be somewhat related to the times when classroom lighting is needed, but not entirely. Some storage will be required, although a smaller capacity than that needed by a wind system whose operation must be considered to be twenty-four hour per day.

The focus here is sustainability, not economics; however, the monetary cost is relevant. It is a reflection of the drain any action has on our ability to resolve problems. We do not have unlimited funds or unlimited time to develop solutions to the energy and environmental crises; therefore, the degree to which we are successful will depend in large part on the cost effectiveness of our solutions. Further, the dollar costs of our actions speak, to a large degree, of the Second Law expenditures they trigger. They are driven by the resources—energy and other—committed in order to transform raw materials into their eventual form. Ultimately, a unified economic structure may describe the complex relationships that exist among environmental, social, cultural, and individual human concerns, but at this point, neither the problem nor the solution has been stated.

Roof monitors, Walt Whitman Birthplace Poetry Center. TSP/Elemental Architecture, 1944.

The direct, local application of a resource will not necessarily lead to its most efficient use. Many aspects of environmentally responsible living require scale, interconnection and interdependency

8.7

Kerosene–Electric Lighting Comparison

There is a tendency to think of stand-alone, independent living patterns as being environmentally preferable to those that rely on large-scale modern technologies. "Getting off of the grid" is presented as a solution to the damages caused by the inappropriate demands placed on utility systems. In fact, unless one is willing to accept profound changes in lifestyle, interconnection will usually produce more efficient and culturally rich conditions. Even with substantial reductions in resource use, most strategies for environmental independence rely on products from an extravagant society, both for technology and for recycled waste materials. Further, even if one is prepared to make these reductions, a pre-industrial self-sufficient strategy requires amounts of land use unsupportable at current population levels. Land is a finite resource.

The efficiency inherent in the application of technology can be seen by comparing the light that is produced by localized, direct conversion of fuel with the light produced by a lamp receiving electricity from a utility grid. There are few consistent sources quantifying the light output from high-performance, direct-fuel-burning light sources; however, an order of magnitude evaluation can be made using statements from the manufacturers of kerosene mantle lamps and lanterns. In each instance, the figures used here for the kerosene

sources are the most optimistic. Manufacturers claim light output for a two-mantle lantern is equivalent to a 75–80 Watt incandescent lamp and a kerosene usage rate of 1 cup (1/16 gallon) per hour. This equates to a source energy commitment of about 8,600 Btu per hour including an allowance of 10 percent for the added energy embodied during the kerosene production.

An 80 Watt lamp will consume 80 Watt-hours per hour or 273 Btu per hour at the building. Assuming an overall efficiency of 25 percent for the generation and distribution of electricity including the added embodied energy in the fuel used at the generator, the incandescent light source equates to a fuel use of about 1,100 Btu per hour or about one eighth that of burning of kerosene.

A 22 Watt compact fluorescent lamp will provide about the same light as an 80 Watt incandescent. This will result in a fuel use at the generator of about 300 Btu per hour or about one thirtieth of the kerosene lantern. Since kerosene can be used to generate electricity, generally in combustion turbine generators that are well suited to heat recovery cogeneration, the comparison of the efficiency of conversion has direct application. (See 5.3, "Incremental Resource Use and the Relationship to Renewables.")

The physical density of cities, which is necessary for the environmental efficiencies characteristic of cities, requires more energy resource than can be collected within the limits of the urban areas themselves. Energy and resource sustainability requires interconnectedness and cooperation.

8.8

Cities, Energy, and Architecture

The architecture of New York City, and therefore the architects and the American Institute of Architects, have been profoundly shaped by energy in all of its manifestations. The converse, that energy has been created and shaped by the city, also holds. Cultural and intellectual energy result from the intense face-to-face opportunities that exist only in the urban situation. Inhabitants and context interchange energy in an ongoing dialogue. But this is about energy in the more commonly understood sense, as in the physical definition of the ability to do work, as in the Laws of Thermodynamics, as in resource delivered by infrastructure.

It seems not coincidental that the age of petroleum, beginning in the mid-nineteenth century, and the founding and growth of the AIA largely parallel each other. The Drake oil well, considered to be the first commercial undertaking of its kind, was drilled in 1859. The Otis Company's first passenger elevator was installed in the Haughwout Building on Broadway and Spring Street in 1857. The Con Ed electric and steam distribution system, a model urban cogeneration network, began in 1882. By the mid 1870s, rapid transit lines were running through parts of Brooklyn. The AIA was founded in New York in 1857.

The modern city only exists through the harnessing of modern energy forms—dense energy. For example, the solar energy that could be collected within a typical Manhattan block—200 by 1000 feet—totals about 20 billion Btu per year. If this were a residential block with 500 dwelling units, it would demand approximately 50 billion Btu of end use energy per year. Clearly, on-site solar energy will not satisfy current urban energy demands.*

Further, the preceding example ignores the fact that if all the solar energy falling on this theoretical block were captured and converted for building use, there would not be daylight, sunlight to support plant growth, and so forth.

Just as the city relies on an immense catchment area for its water needs, its demands for energy far exceed the total of all practical renewable sources within its boundaries. These widened boundaries

* Insolation (solar energy) in New York City averages approximately 425,000 Btu/SF/yr. Assuming an optimistic collection, storage, and conversion efficiency of 25 percent, the solar energy collected on 1 square foot of New York could replace about 100,000 Btu of end-use energy per year. Based on statewide data from the New York State Energy Research and Development Authority and considering the substantial efficiencies of the city, a rough estimate of residential end use energy is 100 million Btu per New York household per year.

may be the result of spatial expansion, as with hydro and wind power, or temporal expansion, as with the fossil fuels that have amassed organic chemical energy over millions of years.

The city's evolution has been driven by and controlled by access to dense sources of energy. Perhaps ironically, this has produced a situation of particularly low per capita energy use. The city is at once energy-dependent and energy-efficient. Despite the fact that the city can not be energy-independent, it remains a highly efficient machine for living. This is synergy.

Why is this so? First and foremost, the city is a three-dimensional system of highly energy-efficient and highly varied interconnected transportation devices. Although horizontal movement generally happens within a relatively shallow stratum—subways, buses, cabs, cars—elevators connect to the ground plane and offer vertical conveyance at every high-rise condition. They are an integral component in a complex intermodal transportation system. The system cannot function without energy resources, but its order, logic, and intensity of use make it possible to carry out life activities using much less energy resource than the alternative, two-dimensional organization based on the private car and diffuse, extended infrastructure. It is the energy density that allows three-dimensional planning and operation, and it is the application of the third dimension that permits the cultural density that is the essence of the contemporary city.

That the city is dependent on a high energy density has long been understood by the architects of the city. The city's architecture speaks to this interdependence. Architects have been innovators in the creation and expressive application of energy capture and technology and have been in the forefront of efforts to use energy more effectively. The New York Chapter of the AIA led the national drive to consider the energy performance of buildings as a fundamental design criterion.* Because of the inescapable interdependencies between the city as a built organism and the natural environment that in its broadest sense is the city's physical context, New York's architects have been profoundly engaged with issues of appropriate, efficient, and effective energy use.

*"Cities, Energy and Architecture" was prepared in 2007 as part of a project organized by Diane Lewis to mark the 150th anniversary of the founding of the American Institute of Architecture.

The edge between the built and
natural environments, New York City.

9

Case Studies

An evaluation of the embodied energy in the Cleveland Trust Tower prepared as part of a campaign to encourage the adaptive reuse of the building rather than its demolition and replacement, showed savings equivalent to more than one and a half million gallons of oil.

9.1

Embodied Energy in the Cleveland Trust Tower

In 2006, Cayuga County in Ohio proposed to demolish and replace a 280,000-square-foot office building in downtown Cleveland. The building, constructed in 1971 as the Cleveland Trust Tower, is currently known as the Ameritrust Tower. In addition to being highly serviceable and embodying significant energy resources, the tower is the only high-rise building in the United States designed by Marcel Breuer. The Breuer tower engages a small but highly prominent Beaux-Arts building by George Post, a turn-of-the-century bank headquarters with an ornate, glass-domed rotunda.

In November 2007, Elemental Architecture was invited by a coalition of Cleveland arts and environmental organizations to analyze the environmental implications of the proposed demolition. Elemental's first comments addressed the cultural and urbanistic environments:

. . . it is about the environmental factors that shape our lives. Whether we understand it on a conscious level or not, whether the manifestation is pictorially literal or conceptually abstract, what we make is very much dependent on our environments, natural and built. As the natural environment has evolved over millennia, the built environment has become what it is today over centuries. We have an obligation to nurture and develop both. This obligation includes protecting the cultural resources that have informed our thinking and our work so that future generations may gain from them.

If the Cleveland Trust Tower were demolished, the city would suffer in so many ways. The 1908 Cleveland Trust Post Rotunda designed by George Post would lose the primary aspect of its physical context and an important part of its historical and cultural context. It would become a detached fragment both in form and in time. Breuer's design, with its modest envelope, avoids competition with the rotunda, in fact gives the rotunda a reason to exist in a twenty-first-century city. If there is concern about the viability of Post's Rotunda, the first step to insure its continued existence is to preserve the tower.

The broad issues of the impact on the natural environment were then reviewed:

Yet however damaging to Cleveland the demolition would be (and it would leave a hole in the city's cultural history as well as wasting tens of millions of the city's and county's dollars), and however damaging it would be to the continuity of American architecture (and it is unquestionably a defining work of one of our finest architects), perhaps most damning would be its example of rampant environmental callousness. This is a very well-conceived and built structure having many decades of useful life remaining.

At a time when we are finally appreciating the impact of excessive energy use on air quality, on global climate change, on our domestic economy, on our international relations, and on our very security, it seems unthinkable to waste millions of gallons of oil to demolish a perfectly serviceable building, a building that many people regard as a highly significant cultural monument, a building that represents important aspects of Cleveland's history, and perhaps one that Cleveland will come to love. It seems unthinkable except for the fact that people are thinking to do exactly that.

A quantified evaluation of the benefits in embodied energy savings followed:

If we look simply at the embodied energy in the building based on generalized square foot numbers, we have a 280,000 square-foot office building embodying a little over 11 gallons of oil (equivalent) per square foot or about 3.2 million gallons of oil. Because these are averages, we could also say that it would take roughly the same embodied energy to replace the building in kind.

But those who want to destroy the building will say that it costs a lot in dollars and in energy to renovate the building. This is true, but will it cost more or less than a comprehensive renovation and upgrade? In order to make an embodied energy comparison between saving the existing building and creating a new one, we need to look at the tower in more detail and estimate the embodied energy of just those components to be saved or, perhaps more importantly, the embodied energy that it would take to replace those components. One way to do this would be to do a detailed take-off of all of the reusable material in the building and apply the energy factors to each, much the same way that one would do a detailed construction cost estimate.

This would give us a very accurate picture, but also would require considerably more time than I was able to devote.

As an alternative, we can look at the breakdown of the new office construction sector and, from that, determine a reasonable estimate of the energy content in the materials that would remain in place.

The largest single energy input comes from the direct use of refined petroleum and electricity at the jobsite. This accounts for about 22 percent of total

embodied energy. Since most of the heavy construction will remain, let's conservatively assume that 60 percent of this embodied energy, about 13 percent of the total, will remain.

The next largest contributor is fabricated structural steel, which accounts for 9.5 percent of total. All of this will remain.

The clay and concrete sector is third, with 7.5 percent of the total. This would include the material for the precast concrete as well as floor slabs and other concrete elements. Let's allow for some repair, retopping of floors, and the like and say that 90 percent of this category can be reused, giving us a reuse of a little under 7 percent of the total. At this point, we have identified about 30 percent of the total embodied energy that will remain in use if the building is restored.

Let's now look at items that we assume will require total replacement. These include sheet-metal work (ducts), nonferrous wire (electric), light fixtures, glass products, refrigeration machinery, paint, elevators, heating equipment, and switchgear (electric again). Together, these items total just under 15 percent. We also said that 40 percent of the jobsite energy or about 9 percent of the total would not be reusable, giving us a total here of 24 percent.

We've now identified 30 percent of the total embodied energy as savable and 24 percent that's not. The remaining 46 percent of the embodied energy is distributed among some 60 miscellaneous categories. We can conservatively say that half of this could be saved and half not, giving us totals of 53 percent of the embodied energy saved and 47 percent requiring replacement, a little better than a fifty-fifty split.

This may not seem like such a good deal, until you remember that we're talking about the total replacement of all mechanical and electrical systems, all of the glazing, most of the interior finishes, new elevators and building controls—essentially a new, high-performance building within the bones and shell of the original, a new high-performance building that respectfully updates the Breuer original, making it eminently viable for decades to come.

These embodied energy savings conservatively work out to be 1.7 million gallons of oil, and Cleveland gets to keep a nationally respected work of architecture. Cleveland also benefits from shorter and less severe demolition and construction disruption. Which raises a point: This analysis has not considered the energy required to demolish the existing building, let alone the environmental issues of disposing of the waste. These would add further benefits to the reuse scenario.

In the summer of 2009, plans to redevelop the building as a hotel and residential condominiums collapsed with the failing real estate market, a poignant reminder that we currently have more built space than program to occupy it.

Shepard Hall is a sprawling, 1907 Gothic Revival structure, the first building erected in New York specifically for public higher education. In 1986, this nationally recognized landmark had deteriorated to such a degree that without comprehensive reconstruction it would have been demolished for safety reasons. In order to reconstruct the envelope, including the total replacement of major structural components, and to preserve the original architectural intent, a program was designed and carried out using the Modernist reliance on systematization, order, and calculated response to clearly articulated problems.

9.2

Shepard Hall

In 1986, George Post's masterpiece, Shepard Hall at City College of New York, had reached such a point of deterioration that serious consideration was given to its demolition. Several areas, including a 35-foot-tall bay window, had already collapsed, and engineering surveys of the main tower and the clerestories of the Great Hall found structural deficiencies severe enough to warrant immediate closure of several large areas of the buildings. More than a third of the 72,000 pieces of ornamental terra cotta had already shattered or been removed out of safety concerns and more than half of the remaining pieces were missing significant pieces, some having been removed as a precaution and some having fallen. The building was surrounded by protective sidewalk sheds.

The most critical reconstruction required the replacement of major building elements, including the entire structure of the four 65-foot-tall turrets at the main tower and, if the architectural character of the building was to be retained, the replacement of about 13,000 pieces of terra cotta. At that time, the largest terra cotta replacement campaign in the United States had replaced fewer than 5,000 pieces

and had been carried out over a twelve year period. Not only was there was no precedent for the work required at Shepard Hall, but the demand for the ornamental replacements exceeded what was then the total domestic production capacity. The reconstruction of the building required the application of Modern design and construction techniques—a concise statement of the problems and goals, an identification of the resources that could be brought to bear, and comprehensive documentation to control publicly bid, lump-sum construction contracting.

The first design criterion was to preserve or re-create the full range of decorative and sculptural elements of George Post's original design. Since the original design's lack of accommodation of thermal movement was identified as a major factor in the original failures, the new solution would have to allow thermal movement of both the overall building and of the individual components. To do this, the decorative replacement pieces were individually supported by the underlying structure, rather than resting on each other. This accomplished three goals. It allowed all of the exterior joints to be elas-

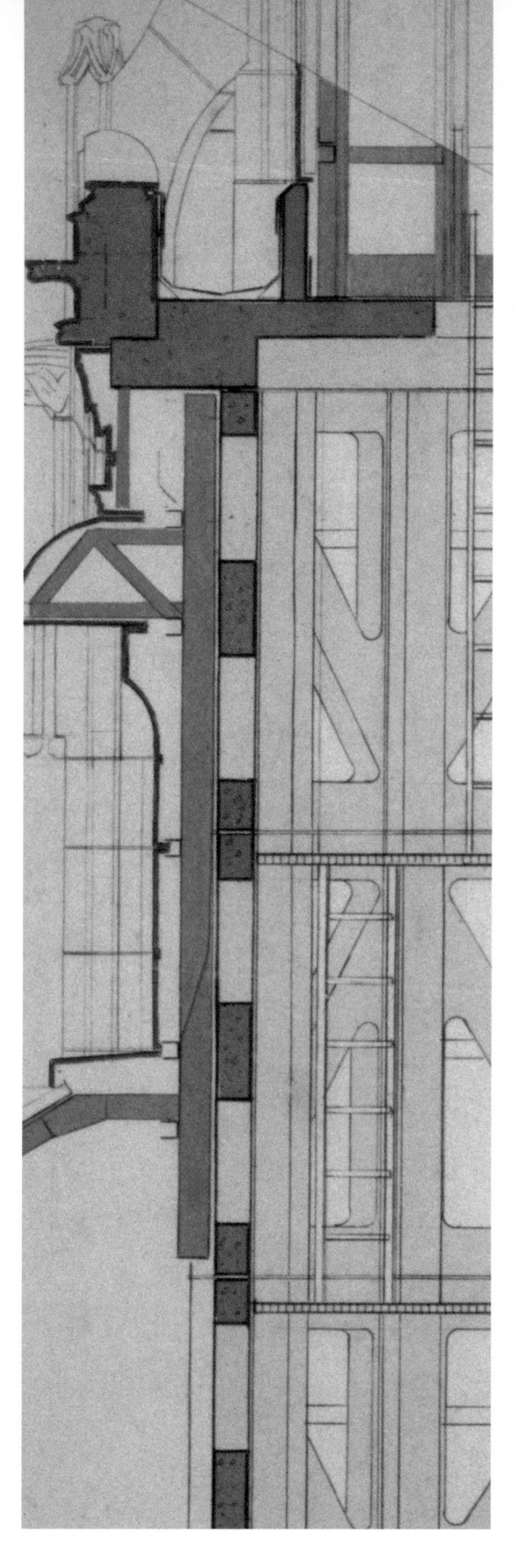

tic, which in turn, accepted a wide range of movement. It permitted the critically important structural reconstruction to proceed on an accelerated schedule, independent from the fabrication and installation of the decorative replacements. Finally, it accommodated future repairs and replacements without compromising the structural integrity of the reconstructed building. In order to carry out this program, the decorative units were remade as thin-shell castings rather than solid masonry blocks.

The solution that separates structure from cladding is predicated on rebuilding the structure, and in most areas the weather enclosure of the building, in a simplified geometric form that fits completely inside the thin-shell assembly. The highly complex thin-shell pieces which exactly replicate the surface shapes of the original terra cotta pieces form what is essentially a rain screen outside the new core. The result is a solution that is Modern in all aspects but one, which is that until one looks behind the surface the rebuilt Shepard Hall appears to be an early-twentieth-century copy of fourteenth-century architecture.

A second aspect critical to realizing the reconstruction was the development of the construction and contract documents. Here, too, the approach was Modernist in its systematization and layered information. The first level of information established the geometry of the substrate, essentially creating a new ground whose form was established to accommodate the inside surfaces of the complex requirements of the new thin-shell replicas (see 8.1.)

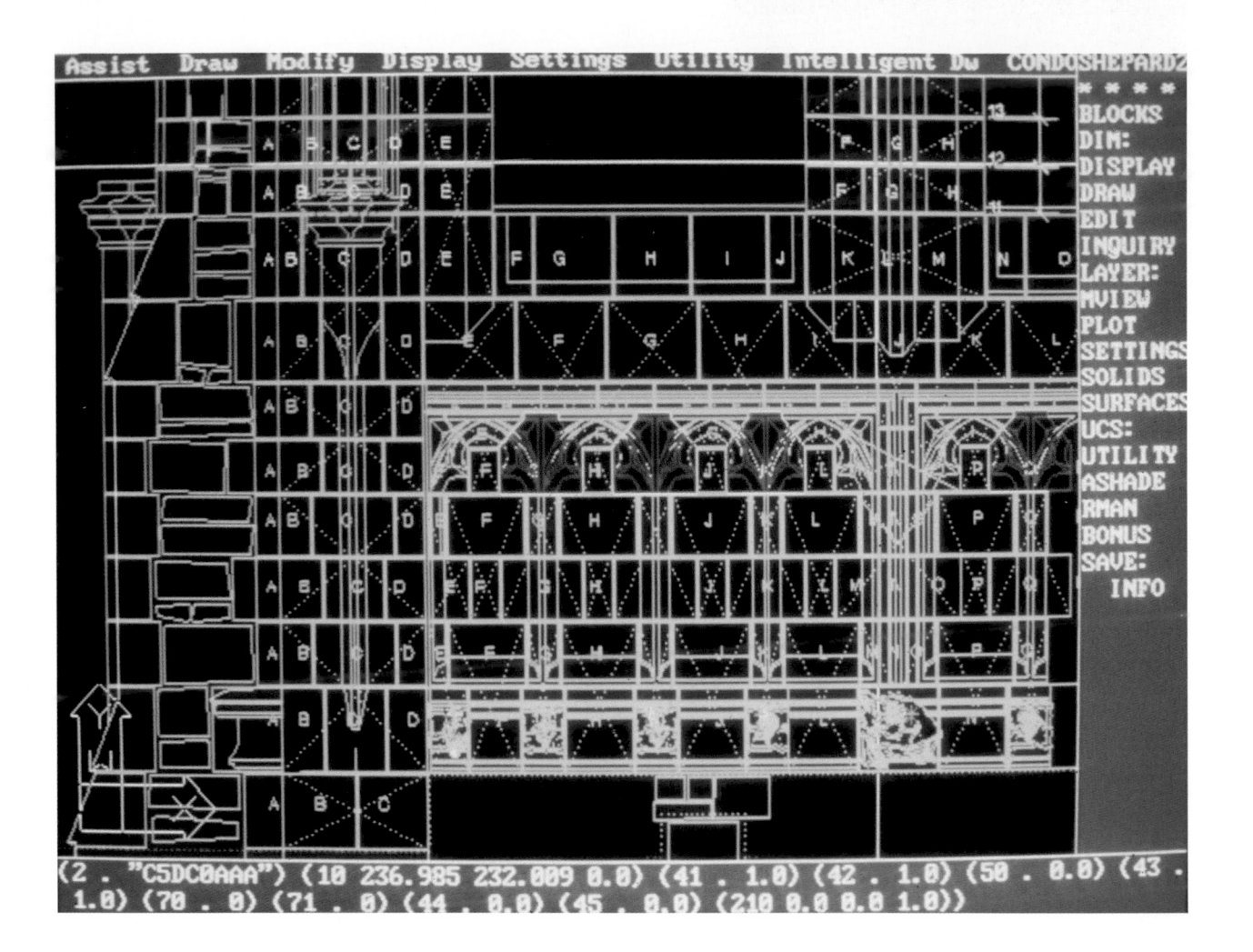

Assist Draw Modify Display Settings Utility Intelligent Dw CONDOSHEPARD2

BLOCKS
DIM:
DISPLAY
DRAW
EDIT
INQUIRY
LAYER:
MVIEW
PLOT
SETTINGS
SOLIDS
SURFACES
UCS:
UTILITY
ASHADE
RMAN
BONUS
SAVE:
INFO

(2 . "C5DC0AAA") (10 236.985 232.009 0.0) (41 . 1.0) (42 . 1.0) (50 . 0.0) (43 .
1.0) (70 . 0) (71 . 0) (44 . 0.0) (45 . 0.0) (210 0.0 0.0 1.0))

opposite

Preliminary study of structure and cladding
system for Main Tower reconstruction
at Shepard Hall, CCNY, New York.
TSP/Elemental Architecture, 1987.

above

Early use of CAD for historic reconstruction project. Shepard Hall II, CCNY,
New York. TSP/Elemental Architecture,
1991.

Once the substrate was defined, the next task was to provide labels or addresses for each of the 72,000 pieces of terra cotta that existed or had once existed on the building. For the first phase, begun in 1986, the drawings were prepared by hand, but the information regarding the 13,000 replacement replicas was managed using a database program, greatly simplifying the layout and tracking of the work through both the design and construction phases. By 1991, when the second phase of work began, the capabilities of computer-based tools had reached a useful level. The drawings were among the first large-scale applications of CAD drawing for historic reconstruction. The drawings and database were linked to provide interconnected graphic and quantified information for materials take-offs and tracking of fabrication and installation. Although most of the areas of the building were hand-measured,

computer-rectified photogrammetry (the reconciliation of multiple photographs to create accurate elevations) allowed recording of parts of the building that could not be accessed without the construction of fixed scaffolding.

The reconstruction of Shepard Hall, allowing it to remain as the architectural symbol of City College, began with the creation of a virtual replica of the original, which was dismantled to develop the strategy and documentation for the actual building. While the virtual exercise was interesting in itself, and tested what were then a number of new and exciting technologies, its real importance was in enabling the realization of the construction and the continued use of the building. No matter how precise, there are significant differences between virtual and physical architecture.

above and opposite

Replica castings and reconstructed turret at Shepard Hall, City College of New York, New York City, George Post, 1907. Reconstruction by TSP/Elemental Architecture, 1986–ongoing.

The South Jamaica Branch Library, which opened in 1999 as part of the Queens Borough Public Library, was the first project built under the High Performance Building Program of the New York City Department of Design and Construction. The building received an inaugural Earth Day Top Ten Award from the national AIA.

9.3

South Jamaica Branch Library

An integrated approach to energy performance with particular emphasis on direct harvesting of solar energy both as light and heat was a significant criterion throughout the design process, beginning with the conceptual and schematic phases.

The program required that the library be built to property lines on three sides leaving only the west exposure, at the street, for openings in the walls. This led to a design which used the roof as the primary source of daylight. The following are excerpts from a pre-schematic report prepared for the client prior to the start of building design.

**NEW SOUTH JAMAICA BRANCH LIBRARY
REPORT ON SUSTAINABLE DESIGN ISSUES
6 MAY 1996**

INTRODUCTION
The development of the design for an environmentally responsive (or sustainable, or "green") building is non-linear and holistic. Each aspect must be reviewed and refined as the overall solution emerges. For the sake of discussion, however, one must look at one element at a time; but in doing so, one must be continuously aware of the complex interrelationships.

For the new South Jamaica Branch Library (SJBL), the environmental issues may first be divided into two broad areas — considerations of operations and conditions within the project boundaries, and the effect of the project on the environment of the rest of the planet. Many of these are connected. For example, reduced fuel use at the building will also reduce the environmental impact of the extraction, processing and transporting of fuel resources.

The major environmental factors which can be affected by design strategies include operating energy requirements, emissions from the building operation, embodied energy in the building itself, indoor air quality effects of material choice, indoor air quality resulting from the design of building systems, material selection to minimize the use of non-renewable resources and resources whose extraction has significant adverse environmental impact.

In order to select the primary targets for these measures, it is first necessary to identify the aspects of building construction and operation which have the greatest impact and, therefore, have the greatest potential for improvement in absolute terms. For operating energy use, although not directly applicable, it is worth looking at a study performed for the Croton-on-Hudson, NY, Public Library, a small, free-standing fully space conditioned building. Approximately 61 percent of the energy used at the site was for space conditioning, 31 percent was for lighting with hot water, pumps and motors, appliances and equipment, and miscellaneous usage requiring less than 10 percent. Clearly, in this case, the potentials for energy savings in space conditioning and lighting far exceed those for any other target. Although this study was performed prior to the wide-spread use of computers, the potential targets which fall within the control of building operation are likely to be similar. For the SJBL, energy performance modeling for various design scenarios will be subject to modeling as the building design evolves.

For indoor air quality, conventional materials with significant off-gassing (release of chemicals) or mechanical deterioration leading to particulate release (dusting or flaking) should be avoided and replaced by more stable materials.

The other element to improving indoor air quality is the control and elimination of problematic substances generated by building use. In a modern library environment, the major objectionable sources are likely to be devices with print output such as copiers, printers, and fax machines. Control of these emissions will greatly improve interior environmental quality.

THERMAL PERFORMANCE—SOLAR ENERGY:
1. Daylighting, Passive Solar Heating, and Cooling Loads
A primary sustainable design goal will be to utilize solar energy for daylighting and passive heating while minimizing cooling requirements during the summer due to over-lighting. Because of the extensive site coverage, it appears likely that the SJBL will have clerestories or monitors, which will result in high "pockets" in the roof/ceiling. This will provide places where hotter air will collect.

During the heating season, a return air system which picks up air at these high points can collect this heated air and redistribute it throughout the building. The distribution of this energy will not only provide immediate heating, it will also heat most of the building mass allowing the building to "coast" into the late afternoon and evening when there is little or no solar energy available.

During the cooling season, most of the building exhaust requirements can be taken from these high points with return air for the system taken low in the building. This will reduce the requirements for mechanical cooling while maintaining a good air exchange rate.

2. Background

The constructive utilization of solar energy will fall into two primary areas, daylighting and direct solar heat gain during the heating season. These are closely interrelated. Most sunlight entering the building will eventually become heat. The exception is that portion of the light that is reflected and passes back through the glazed areas of the building without being absorbed. During the heating season, solar energy entering the building (generally as light) will become heat and will reduce the demand on the heating system. During the cooling season, solar energy entering the building will place a load on the cooling system; however, if this solar energy is providing necessary light, the resulting load on the cooling system will be approximately the same as that which would be caused by an electric lighting system. Thus, it can be seen that, from a lighting point of view, there will be overall energy savings if whenever the building is in use, available solar energy can reduce or eliminate the need to use electricity for lighting. A related issue is whether this introduction of solar energy for lighting can have other benefits (such as for space heating), or whether there are some related energy costs (such as added cooling loads). Where there is added benefit, this should be maximized. Where there are associated costs, care must be used to introduce only the required amounts of daylight so that costs are minimized. From a gross energy balance viewpoint, this suggests several design goals.

3. Heating Season

During the heating season, some degree of "over-lighting" with sunlight (that is, providing light levels above minimum standards) in order to maximize heat gain is desirable up to the point that the light environment is excessively bright. In doing this, it is important to provide the control to prevent direct sunlight from reaching work surfaces or hitting occupants. This can be achieved using a combination of specular (mirror-like) and non-specular (matt or diffusing) reflectors. For example, a specular exterior louver can direct a beam of sunlight through a window to a light colored (white) non-specular ceiling surface that will distribute the light over a wide area of the interior.

Where light levels become too high for comfort or effective work, dark absorptive surfaces within the building can capture solar energy directly as heat. This is a less complete utilization of solar energy than the combination of daylight to heat; however it will still offset the need for using non-renewable, emission causing energy sources for heating.

In order to utilize passive solar gain for heating, whether combined with daylighting or heat only, it is necessary to distribute the heat from where it is collected to where it is needed, and to store it to smooth out temperature fluctuations as the sun angle and cloud cover change. Within the library, solar heat must be collected and stored at temperatures that are within a pre-determined comfort range. The storage of large amounts

of heat energy requires either large amounts of material or material with a high thermal storage density (such as water or stone). One approach is to make use thermally "heavy" materials throughout the building and then distribute the solar heat, thus storing the heat at its eventual point of use. The amount of solar heat that would raise the air (very low thermal mass) in a room 20 degrees might only raise the floor and walls 5 degrees. In the first case, the room would be unpleasantly hot but in the second it might be perfectly comfortable. An added advantage to the storage of heat at a relatively low temperature is that the rate of heat loss is a function of the temperature difference across the enclosure. Storing thermal energy at lower temperatures reduces the rate of loss to the outside environment.

4. Cooling Season
During the cooling season, it will be desirable to avoid over-lighting in order to minimize the loads on the cooling system. Daylighting to some predetermined level will result in about the same cooling load as relatively efficient electric lighting. The problems typically associated with daylighting and cooling are, first, that it is easy to provide much higher light levels with daylight than with electric sources and, second, that electric lighting systems are often operated in spaces and at times when daylight is completely adequate thereby resulting in excess energy, and consequently heat, being introduced into that space.

In order to minimize potential overheating during cooling seasons, the amount of sunlight introduced into to space should be limited to that amount necessary to provide appropriate light levels. In all seasons, lights should not be on when daylight is adequate.

5. Approach
The heating and cooling "system" for the New South Jamaica Branch Library includes the building itself and the mechanical HVAC components, and the lighting/shading systems. Each depends on the other.

THERMAL PERFORMANCE-BUILDING ENVELOPE
1. General Criteria
The shell of the new South Jamaica Branch Library will provide a high level of control of thermal transfer. At times when heat gain or loss increases the load on energy-consuming systems, this control will be directed at minimizing thermal transfer. That is, thermal conductance and radiation will be minimized, and exchange of inside and outside air will be limited to that required for ventilation. At times when heat gain or loss helps to maintain the desired interior conditions, this control will maximize the desirable transfer.

Conductance is controlled by insulation. Radiation is controlled primarily by the glazing material. Air exchange is controlled by overall envelope lightness, door and window construction and entrance planning allowing modulation of the HVAC system to determine the air change rates.

At times two criteria may suggest contradictory envelope conditions. For example, during the winter it will be desirable to minimize heat loss from the building while maximizing the solar heat gain in order to reduce the load on the heating system. Opaque envelope materials can have significantly better insulating properties than the highest performing transparent surfaces. For a strictly thermal evaluation, it is necessary to find the optimal balance between beneficial solar gain and control of thermal loss. The equation is further complicated by the potential for energy savings resulting from utilizing daylight, as well as from the less quantifiable benefits of the spatial and psychological qualities of a daylighted facility.

2. Building Form

The building will be designed to capture solar energy with control of absorption and reflection, and of total input. The transfer of solar energy into the building occurs at the building envelope. For the new South Jamaica Branch Library, more than half of the above-grade envelope will be the roof. Further, three of the four facades are either at the property line or so close to the property line that access to the sun on these walls can not be insured. The roof form will be articulated to permit solar capture, both for heating and lighting. That is to say, there will be monitors, clerestories, skylights or other features which will create high pockets in the ceilings as well as entry points for solar energy. Because of the natural tendency for hot air to rise, it will collect in these pockets where it may be col-

lected and recirculated when desired, and rejected when cooling is needed. This pattern of operation suggests several considerations for the roof design.

The shape of the ceiling/roof should "channel" the hot air to the point of collection. This is important because the temperature differential driving the hot air toward these collection points will be relatively small so smooth and directed paths will maximize the quantities of hot air brought to these pockets. This will benefit the cooling as well as the heating. Any heat that is directly rejected will reduce the load on the chillers.

The high "pockets" should be sized and shaped to concentrate the hot air. During the cooling season, if the demand for outside air is relatively small, the air that is exhausted should carry out as much heat as possible.

The collection "pockets" should be well insulated so that during the heating season, conducted heat loss will be minimized. Because even high performance glass will have conducted heat loss rates that are 4 to 10 times higher than a well insulated opaque surface, the it may be desirable to provide opaque "pockets" above the glazed roof areas.

MECHANICAL SYSTEMS

The mechanical system or systems used to augment the heating and cooling must, during the heating season, be able to capture the solar-derived heat which will be only slightly higher (+/- 10°F) in temperature than the ambient temperatures

and distribute it to storage media, preferably the building mass itself. During the cooling season, the system will reject directly as much heat as is possible without returning it to the portion of the system providing chilled air.

There are several types of HVAC systems that could distribute the energy as described above. These systems include ducted heated and cooled air; heated and chilled water with an air-to-water (or glycol) heat exchanger to capture heat from the space; a composite system utilizing small package heating and cooling units and a separate exhaust among others.

The mechanical system must be appropriate to the non-mechanical behavior of the building, be simple to operate and maintain, and be efficient in its overall operation.

DAYLIGHTING

Along with space conditioning, the other major potential for reduced energy consumption is the utilization of daylighting in lieu of electric lights. As noted above, this is integrally related to the heating and cooling requirements for the building.

During the winter, daylight brought into the building will also reduce the load on the heating system.

During the summer, daylight will introduce about the same load on the cooling system as will electric light providing the same levels of illumination.

This last qualification is important because of the fact that, using daylight, it is easy to achieve much higher than minimal. Therefore, if daylighting levels are not controlled, excessive loads may be imposed on the cooling systems.

It goes without saying that daylighting will only result in energy savings if electric lights are not used when sunlight is available. A photosensitive control system will be provided that will modulate the electric lights in response to daylighting conditions.

A primary consideration in design for daylighting is avoiding conditions where direct solar beams can strike work surfaces. Additionally, it is not desirable to have direct sunlight on wall surfaces which are in the primary field of view of visitors or staff. Within the space, sunlight should be diffuse. This can be accomplished by a diffusing filter — frosted glass for example — or by a diffusing reflector such as a matte white surface. There are several advantages of the reflector approach.

Direct sunlight can be brought more deeply into a space and then diffused, providing greater coverage.

When solar energy is diffused at the exterior glazing, a significant portion of the solar energy is directed to the exterior. Even where daylighting remains adequate, the solar energy available for heating will be reduced.

South Jamaica Branch Library.
TSP/Elemental Architecture, 1999.

As noted above, appropriate levels of daylighting will have little negative impact on cooling loads. This, however, requires that excessive sunlight be rejected during cooling seasons. For south facing glass, a system of fixed-bladed horizontal louvers can be set to allow the direct passage of low winter sunlight while reflecting the higher summer sun. If the blades or non-specular (matte), a portion of the reflection will be away from the building thus reducing the amount of entering solar energy. These blades can be shallow and closely spaced providing the added benefit of security.

A specular interior reflector can be coupled with the non-specular exterior louver. Where the sun angle permits direct solar rays to enter the building, this interior reflector will direct the light against a matte surface which will act as a diffuser. This combination of reflectors will seasonally control the amount of daylight entering the space, distribute daylight throughout the space, and deliver diffuse light to the areas of use.

CONTROLS

During the design process, the possibility of using a PC-based building energy management system will be reviewed. Until recently, such a system would not have been appropriate for a project of this size; however, new programs and more reliable equipment make this an approach worth careful consideration. A key factor in the decision will be whether there is a clear presentation or reporting of the effects of specific instructions and/or operating routines on building system operation and overall building behavior. For example, in shifting to heating mode, the operation of fans and dampers to recirculate the collected hot air from the building high points should be apparent.

One advantage of utilizing PC-based control system is that multiple functions can be interrelated. Because the system is so powerful, however, care must be taken to avoid over complicating the operation to the point that the human operators do not understand what the controls are doing or what they are responding to.

Another advantage of a PC-based system for a demonstration project is that operational patterns can be easily recorded and studied.

EMBODIED ENERGY

The embodied energy* in typical library construction is approximately 1.3 million Btu per square foot. The on site energy required to operate a highly efficient library building might be about 35,000 Btu per square foot per year which translates to a source energy** consumption of about 80,000 Btu per square foot per year. The energy required to build the library will be approximately equivalent to the energy that is required for about seventeen years. In other words, a thirty percent savings in the embodied energy for construction would be like getting five energy-free years of operation.

* Embodied energy refers to the total quantity of energy required to extract and process raw materials, manufacture finished materials and assemblies, transport them to the building site, prepare the site and assemble the components and materials in the field. Data are taken from *the Handbook of Energy Use for Building Construction.*

** Source energy takes into account the loss of efficiency in the conversion of basic energy resources (crude oil, coal, etc.) into useful service within the building envelope. For example, each kW of electric energy used within the building will require the commitment of about four kW (13.6 thousand Btu) of basic energy resources.

Embodied energy requirements can be reduced in two ways. There are materials with lower embodied energy that can be substituted for high embodied energy materials; and buildings can be designed to use less materials. Both of these options will be explored and quantified in the design for the new SJBL.

INDOOR AIR QUALITY

We are becoming increasingly aware of problems associated with the release of noxious or toxic gasses from materials for extended time periods after their manufacture (off-gassing). Where these materials are used on the interiors of buildings, conditions have ranged from being unpleasant to being severely unhealthy. In general, polymers and solvent-based products have exhibited the greatest problems with off-gassing, either because they are inherently unstable, because they have recently undergone some chemical transformation which is not yet fully resolved, or because a volatile (and objectionable) material which has been used in production has not fully evaporated. Frequently, natural materials, such as cotton, wool, wood, etc., have been used to address the problems associated with synthetics. While this reduces or eliminates off-gassing, other problems such as hosting fungi and insects may arise. This has been particularly a problem with some natural carpet backing materials. Chemical treatment of natural products to control growth of fungi may cause emissions that are more objectionable than those from synthetics.

Care must also be taken to avoid materials which require cleaning and maintenance products which release objectionable or dangerous substances.

As the SJBL project progresses, a palette of interior materials will be developed and discussed with the intention of providing a system that will introduce as little objectionable emission to the building interior as is possible.

A second major area of concern regarding indoor air quality is the emissions resulting from the program activities of the library. One major class of these sources is devices with printers including copiers, fax machines, and printers and plotters. If possible, these devices should be clustered and provided with localized exhaust preferably having direct discharge from the building. This may not be practical or may result in a significantly increased load on the heating and cooling systems to condition excess incoming outside air. In this case, the air collected at the printers must be to filtered prior to recirculation. In either case, however, the emissions from this equipment should not be allowed to mix freely with the air within the space.

In addition to the equipment, there may be activities in the library which use solvents or solvent-based materials, such as rubber cement, acetone or spray coatings, and adhesives. If this is anticipated, a defined area with special exhaust should be provided, first to reduce exposure of the staff to these materials and second to prevent the spread of these materials into the rest of the building.

opposite
Light shelf and diffuser baffle,
South Jamaica Branch Library.
TSP/Elemental Architecture, 1999.

A Way Forward

In the United States, there is a huge inventory of unused, underused, and poorly configured buildings, many of them modern-style. These buildings are a valuable resource, and until this resource has been exhausted, the pace and pattern of new building construction seen in the second half of the twentieth century is a luxury that is not sustainable. There are also numerous modern-style buildings which are highly wasteful in their use of operating resources, particularly energy and water. Their continued operation with poor efficiencies is not sustainable.

To be clear, sustainability references a future in which our children and grandchildren *can exist* and in which they will *want to exist*. Given humankind's incredible power to affect the natural environment, survival of the species is no longer an academic question. As a result, the issue of global sustainability might more appropriately be called survivability. Climate change, limits on food production, and availability of clean water and air threaten the continued viability of the human species. Because the problems are real and the stakes are high, it is often difficult for environmentalists, particularly those working on national and international matters, to take into account those factors which do not directly impact survival—the *can exist* issues. However, in addressing questions of survival, it is important that we not lose sight of *want to exist* concerns, which define and enrich human experience, such as the enjoyment of beaches and sunsets, trees and flowers, and animals and birds, as well as appreciation of our cultural heritages and histories.

In scale, *can exist* concerns may be seen as global whereas *want to exist* concerns are generally local. The relevance of the different scales brings to mind the mantra "think globally, act locally" (the application of which to environmental concerns is generally attributed to Dr. Rene Dubos). However, a more holistic view suggests that this be rephrased as "think globally, think locally and act at whatever scale opportunity presents itself." That is, the conceptualization and understanding of sustainability must occur simultaneously at macro and micro levels in order to incorporate the complexities whose synergies are at the heart of any comprehensive ecological program.

Increasingly, we are finding resonances between maintenance of place, of genius loci, and global ecological survival. These result from several fundamental conditions. Much of what is valued by humankind is the result of a long, evolutionary process in which the growth and development of habitation of the planet has been informed by interaction with context. Understanding the intrinsic value of what currently exists produces attitudes which are far more likely to embrace adapting and reusing, rather than demolishing and replacing—an integral aspect of any sustainable planning effort.

It is interesting to note that the global/local precept was an underlying idea of Patrick Geddes's 1915 work *Cities in Evolution*. In addition to the influence exerted by his own writing, the Scottish biologist and proto-ecologist had a profound influence on social and environmental leaders including Lewis Mumford and Barry Commoner, particularly as he discussed the interrelationship between built form and solutions to social problems. It is also interesting that, although Geddes's earlier work is generally associated with pre-Raphaelites and particularly John Ruskin, his later view of the interconnections between social and spatial phenomena—namely, that planning and building design are inextricably tied to the larger ecosystem as well as to social and cultural patterns—informs and is informed by Modernism. By extension, it is apparent that the integrative holism essential to Modernism must also be fundamental to any meaningful program for comprehensive sustainability, and that resources

must be used directly, in their highest state. However, the inevitable conclusion that existing rather than new structures must be the primary means for meeting the bulk of our programmatic needs should not be seen as either reactionary or a movement toward reduced quality of life. To the contrary, increased use of existing buildings, and the associated reduction in new construction, offers several important cultural benefits and also produces more jobs per dollar. Extended use of the building inventory reinforces an important physical component of our cultural continuum. Elimination of casually commissioned new construction increases recognition of the cultural value of those new buildings determined to be necessary.

Recently, we have seen the proliferation of physical replicas of landmark buildings and locales. This has dramatically increased the level of cultural background noise, of cultural entropy. At the same time, we have seen ecologically and economically vulnerable elements of our world threatened and destroyed by pressures for expansion and growth. Some of these pressures arise from the need to meet very legitimate demands, but many do not. Regardless, authentic places are becoming ever more precious, and the imperative to reuse resources at their highest Second Law value is a strong pragmatic argument for the preservation of these places.

While Modernism resulted in large part from capabilities that occurred only with the availability

of large quantities of energy, it was also an intense investigation into cultural and social questions associated with the new technologies. The time-frames of both the petroleum era and the advent of Modernism are interdependent, yet recent enough that we are just beginning to place these two phenomena in a common framework. The Modern movement is about one hundred years old. It is just one hundred and fifty years since the beginning of commercial extraction of petroleum. Related to the history of human culture, it is essentially irrelevant whether oil will run out in twenty-five, fifty, or one hundred years. The Paleolithic cave paintings in Lascaux, France have been dated to approximately 14,000 BCE. Sumerian written culture began about 5,500 years ago, with intensive agriculture starting nearly 2,000 years earlier. The origins of the Xia dynasty in China are about 4,000 years old. The Greco-Roman traditions of art and architecture started more than 2,500 years ago, yet much of contemporary Western culture is a manifestation of a continuous evolution from these foundations. This is to say that both the petroleum era and the Modern movement are brief blips on the timeline of the human species. With remarkable shortsightedness, we have come to believe that the petroleum-era paradigm, which was made possible by the availability of plentiful cheap energy, represents the natural order. In fact, it is not sustainable and it is tending toward catastrophic results.

At the same time that the widespread use of petroleum was changing economics, technology, and production, Modernism was formulating a set of ideas and processes to access the benefits inherent in this usage and to address the problems that it created. In considering its potential as a basis for planning and architecture in the context of finite resources, it is critical that Modernism not be seen as a style or a body of work based on style. That certain groups of Modern buildings are similar in appearance does not result from the casual application of stylistic features, but rather from carefully considered responses to a common set of problems resolved in a particular cultural and historical period. Our context is characterized by the realization that essential resources are absolutely finite and by the corollary that sustainability in its broadest sense must be a primary criterion in the allocation of all finite resources. The immense impact on resource use inherent in planning and architecture, and the analytic structures integral to Modernism which provide an armature for design based on context, offer a way forward.

Bibliography

NOTE: This bibliography includes both works cited in this book as well as suggested further reading on the connections between Modern thought and sustainability. Because of its rate of change, information on current technologies is best researched using sources which are frequently updated, the Internet in particular.

Bahamón, Alejandro, and Maria Camila Sanjinés. *Rematerial*. New York: W. W. Norton, 2010.

Banham, Reyner. *Theory and Design of the First Machine Age*. Boston, MA: MIT Press, 1960.

Commoner, Barry. *Science and Survival*. New York: The Viking Press, 1967.

Conrads, Ulrich*, ed. Programs and Manifestoes on 20th-Century Architecture*. MIT: MIT Press, 1975.

Fuller, R. Buckminster. *Operating Manual for Spaceship Earth*. New York: Dutton, 1963.

Gatje, Robert. *Marcel Breuer: A Memoir*. New York: Monacelli Press, 2000.

Geddes, Patrick. *Cities in Evolution*. London: Williams & Norgate, 1915.

Gropius, Walter. *Scope of Total Architecture*. 1954. New York: Collier Books, 1962.

Hyman, Isabelle. *Marcel Breuer, Architect*. New York: Abrams, 2001.

Le Corbusier. *La Charte d'Athenes*. Paris: Plon, 1943. Translated by Anthony Eardley as *The Athens Charter*. New York: Grossman Publishers, 1973.

Le Corbusier. *Vers Une Architecture. Paris: G. Cres, 1923.* Translated by Frederick Etchells as *Towards a New Architecture*. London: John Rodker, 1927.

McHarg, Ian L. *Design With Nature*. New York: Natural History Press, 1969.

Meadows, Donella H. *The Limits to Growth*. New York: Signet, 1972.

Mumford, Lewis. *Myth of the Machine: Technics and Human Development*. New York: Harcourt, 1967.

Papanek, Victor. *The Green Imperative: Ecology and Ethics in Design and Architecture*. New York: Thames and Hudson, 1995.

Schumacher, E.F. *Small is Beautifu: Economics as if People Mattered*. London: Frederick Muller Ltd., 1973.

Stein, Carl. *Energy Conscious Architecture*. Washington, DC: National Council of Architectural Registration Boards, 1993.

Stein, Richard G. *Architecture and Energy*. Garden City, NY: Anchor Press, 1977.

Stein, Richard G. and Carl Stein. *Handbook of Energy Use for Building Construction*. Springfield, VA: National Technical Information Service, 1981.

Sullivan, Chip. *Garden and Climate*. New York: McGraw-Hill, 2002.

Index